D1599942

AMERICAN CARDINAL READERS

For Catholic Parochial Schools

BOOK FOUR

EDITOR OF UPPER GRADE READERS

T. ADRIAN CURTIS, A.B., LL.B.

District Superintendent, formerly Principal, Alexander Hamilton
Junior High School, New York

EDITOR OF LOWER GRADE READERS

EDITH M. McLAUGHLIN

Former Critic Teacher, Parker Practice School,
Normal School, Chicago, Ill.

ASSOCIATE EDITORS

SISTER MARY AMBROSE, O.S.D., A.M.
(Supervisor)
St. Joseph's College and Academy,
Adrian, Michigan

SISTER MARY GERTRUDE, A.M.
Former Supervisor of Parochial High Schools
Sisters of Charity, Convent Station,
New Jersey

SISTER JAMES STANISLAUS
Former Supervisor of Parochial Schools,
Sisters of St. Joseph of Carondolet, St. Louis

ARTHUR H. QUINN, PH.D., LITT.D.
Professor of English, University of
Pennsylvania

REPUBLISHED BY
THE NEUMANN PRESS
LONG PRAIRIE, MINNESOTA

BY SPECIAL ARRANGEMENT WITH
BENZIGER PUBLISHING COMPANY
NEW YORK, CINCINNATI, CHICAGO, SAN FRANCISCO
PRINTERS TO THE HOLY APOSTOLIC SEE

Nihil Obstat
ARTHUR J. SCANLAN, S.T.D.
Censor Librorum

Imprimatur
† PATRICK CARDINAL HAYES
Archbishop of New York

NEW YORK, APRIL 27, 1929

ISBN 0-911845-39-9
THIS 1996 EDITION IS PUBLISHED THROUGH SPECIAL ARRANGEMENT WITH
BENZIGER PUBLISHING COMPANY BY
THE NEUMANN PRESS
LONG PRAIRIE, MINNESOTA

TO THE BOYS AND GIRLS OF OUR CATHOLIC SCHOOLS

All boys and girls love stories. Many of you may remember how you used to ask to have stories told to you at home before you were old enough to go to school. You liked to hear the "Mother Goose Rhymes," over and over again; you enjoyed stories about animals, "The Greedy Dog and the Bone," "The Fox and the Grapes"; you were thrilled by the brave and good deeds of boys and girls who had lived long ago. After your school days began, the pleasantest part of the day for most of the pupils was the time when your teacher told you stories.

Now, after three years of school work, you are able to read fairly long stories by yourselves. At home, in the evening, after lessons have been done, instead of asking Father or Mother to tell you a story, you can get your story-book and enjoy a quiet hour of reading. Because you are able to do this, your reading lessons in school will undergo a change. You must begin to understand the difference between silent reading and reading aloud. Most of your reading outside of school will be done silently. Only now and again will you find an occasion to read aloud.

When you read silently, you are reading for yourselves, either to gain knowledge or for amusement. When you read aloud, you are reading to give the subject matter to others. Silent reading requires speed. The more rapidly you read, the clearer will be the understanding of the ideas contained in the selection. Oral reading requires clearness of expression. You must get the meaning of what you read, not only for yourselves, but you must also express those thoughts in such a way that your listeners will understand the subject matter. The clearness of your speech and the expression given to your utterances become most important.

The selections in these readers will have to be read and studied by you in a variety of ways. Some of them will be read silently for the facts of knowledge that you must get from them. For example, there are pieces about your holy religion that contain facts that you must think about and talk about and remember. There are stories about far-away places that will give you information that will aid you in your study of geography and history. There are selections about animals and plants that will help you in your nature study work.

Another group of selections it is necessary to read aloud in a special manner in order to bring out their beauty. For example, you will more fully appreciate the poetry in this reader if you can read it with the proper expression and rhythm. The prose stories that you will read for entertainment will give you an increased enjoyment if they are read aloud.

If then, during these three intermediate years, you will study these selections, in accordance with the directions of your teachers, you will not only become good readers but you will also be building a firm foundation for your higher studies.

THE EDITORS

ACKNOWLEDGMENTS

For permission to use copyright material grateful acknowledgment is made to Miss Zoe Akins for "First Rain;" to Milton Bradley & Co. for "The Minstrel's Song" by Maud Lindsay from *Mother Stories*, "Nahum Prince" by Edward Everett Hale from *Stories Children Need* by Carolyn Sherwin Bailey, "The Vision of Sir Launfal" by Lawton B. Evans from *Worthwhile Stories for Every Day;* to Thomas Y. Crowell Co. for the adaptation "Moni and the Goats" from *Moni the Goat Boy* by Johanna Spyri; to Dodd, Mead & Company for "A Child's Evensong" by Richard le Gallienne from *English Poems;* to Harper & Brothers for "A Tragic Story" by William Makepeace Thackeray from *Ballads and Tales* and "A Mad Tea Party" from *Alice in Wonderland* by Lewis Carroll; to Houghton Mifflin Company for "The Sermon of St. Francis," "Hiawatha's Childhood" and "The Children's Hour" from *Longfellow's Complete Poetical Works*, for "A Canoe Trip Down the Mississippi" by Eva March Tappan from *American History Stories for Very Young People*, "Pine Tree Shillings" from *Grandfather's Chair* by Nathaniel Hawthorne and "Bird Travels" by Olive Thorne Miller from *First Book of Birds;* to Little, Brown & Co. for "The Legend of St. Christopher" by Helen Hunt Jackson; to Francis A. Litz for "Christopher Columbus" from *The Poetry of Father Tabb* published by Dodd, Mead & Company; to David McKay Co. for "The Wind and the Moon" by George MacDonald; to The Macmillan Company for "The Loaves and Fishes" and "The Marriage

Feast'' from *A Week with Christ the King* by Sister Mary Gertrude, ''The Basque Song'' from *A Catholic Anthology* by Thomas Walsh, ''The Story of Christopher Columbus'' by Elizabeth Harrison from *In Storyland* and ''Apple Blossoms'' by William Martin from *By Way of Mountains* in King's Highway Series; to John Murray (London) for ''Gay Robin'' by Robert Bridges from *Poetical Works;* to Charles Scribner's Sons for ''Autumn Fires'' by Robert Louis Stevenson, ''The Sugar Plum Tree'' by Eugene Field from *Writings in Prose and Poetry,* ''The Wonderful Tar Baby'' by Joel Chandler Harris from *Evening Tales,* ''The Clocks of Rondaine'' by Frank R. Stockton from *Fanciful Tales,* and ''Song of Summer'' by Mary Mapes Dodge from *Rhymes and Jingles.*

CONTENTS

vii

THE RAISING OF THE FLAG

Lift up the banner of the stars,
The standard of the double bars,
Red with the holy tide
Of heroes' blood, who died
At the feet of liberty,
Shouting her battle-cry
Triumphantly
As they fell like sickled corn
In that first resplendent morn
Of freedom, glad to die
In the dawn of her clear eye!

Lift up the banner red
With the blood of heroes shed
In victory!
Lift up the banner blue
As heaven, and as true
In constancy!

Lift up the banner white
As sea foam in the light
Of liberty;
The banner of the triple hue,
The banner of the red and white and blue,
Bright ensign of the free!

Lift up your hearts to Him who made to shine
In Heaven's arch the glorious sign
Of mercy's heavenly birth
To all the peoples of the earth,
The pledge of peace divine!
And let our glorious banner, too,
The banner of the rainbow's hue,
In Heaven's wide expanse unfurled,
Be for a promise to the world
Of peace to all mankind;
Banner of peace and light,
Banner of red and blue and white,
Red as the crimson blood
Of Christ's wide brotherhood,
Blue with the unchanging hope
Of Heaven's steadfast sun,
White as the radiant sun,
The whole earth shining on!

THE ANGEL OF THE RESURRECTION

Angel of man's Redeemer, weep no more!
I come with comforts for sad hearts and sore.
    This little Child shall gain
        All men's hearts as their King;
    He shall arise and reign
        Almighty, triumphing!

I shall roll back the great tomb's rocky door;
I shall behold His Lovely Face once more;
    And I shall sing,
        And I shall then rejoice
    When I shall see my King,
        And hear again His voice.

3

THE STORY OF CHRISTOPHER COLUMBUS

Once upon a time, far across the great ocean, there lived a little boy named Christopher. The city in which he lived was called Genoa. It was on the coast of the great sea, and from the time that little Christopher could first remember, he had seen boats come and go across the water. I doubt not that he had little boats of his own which he tried to sail or paddle on the small pools near his home.

Soon after he was old enough to read books, which in those days were very scarce and very much valued, he got hold of an account of the wonderful travels of a man named Marco Polo. Over and over again little Christopher read the marvelous stories told by this old traveler, of the strange cities which he had seen and of the dark-colored people whom he had met; of the queer houses; of the wild and beautiful animals he had encountered; of the jewels and perfumes and flowers which he had come across.

All day long the thoughts of little Christopher were busy with this strange far-away land which Marco Polo described. All night long he dreamed of the marvelous sights to be seen on those distant

4

shores. Many a time he went down to the water's edge to watch the queer ships as they slowly disappeared in the dim distance, where the sea and sky seemed to meet. He listened eagerly to everything about the sea and the voyages of adventure or of trade which were told by the sailors near by.

When he was fourteen years old, he went to sea with an uncle who was commander of one of the vessels that came and went from the port of Genoa. For a number of years he thus lived on a vessel, learning everything that he could about the sea. At one time the ship on which he was sailing had a desperate fight with another ship; both took fire and were burned to the water's edge.   Christopher Columbus, for that was his full name, escaped, as did the other sailors, only by jumping into the sea and swimming ashore.   Still this did not cure him of his love for the ocean life.

We find that after a time he left Italy, his native country, and went to live in Portugal, a land near the great sea, whose people were far more venturesome than had been those of Genoa.   Here he married a beautiful maiden, whose father had collected a rich store of maps and charts, which showed what was then supposed to be the shape of the earth, and told of strange and wonderful voyages which brave soldiers had from time to time dared to make out into the then unknown sea.   Most people in those days thought it was certain death to any one who ventured very far out on the ocean.

There were all sorts of queer and absurd ideas afloat as to the shape of the earth.   Some people thought it was round and flat like a pancake and that the waters which surrounded the land gradually changed into mist and vapor, and that he who ventured out into these vapors fell through the mist and clouds down into—they knew not where.   Others believed that there were huge monsters living in the distant waters, ready to swallow any sailor who was foolish enough to venture near them.

But Christopher Columbus had grown to be a very wise and thoughtful man and from all he could learn from the maps of his father-in-law and the books which he read, and from the long talks which he had with some other learned men, he grew more and more certain that the world was round like an orange, and that by sailing westward from the coast of Portugal one could gradually go round the world and find at last the wonderful land of Cathay, the strange country which lay far beyond the sea, the accounts of which had so thrilled him as a boy.

We, of course, know that he was right in his belief concerning the shape of the earth, but people in those days laughed him to scorn when he spoke of making a voyage out on the vast and fearful ocean. In vain he talked and reasoned and argued, and drew maps to explain matters. The more he proved to his own satisfaction that this must be the shape of the world, the more people shook their heads and called him crazy.

He remembered in his readings of the book of Marco Polo's travels that the people whom he had met were heathens, who knew little about the dear

God who made the world, and nothing at all about his Son, Christ Jesus; and as Christopher Columbus loved very dearly the Christian religion, his mind became filled with a great longing to carry it across the great seas to that far-away country. The more he thought about it, the more he wanted to go, until his whole life was filled with the one thought of how to get hold of some ships to prove that the earth was round, and that these far-away heathens could be reached.

Through some friends he obtained admission to the court of the King of Portugal. Eagerly he told the rich monarch of the great enterprise which filled his heart. It was of little or no use; the King was busy with other affairs, and only listened to the words of Columbus as one might listen to the wind. Year after year passed by; Columbus' wife had died, and their one little son, Diego, had grown to be quite a boy. Finally Columbus decided he would leave Portugal and would go over to Spain, a rich country near by, and see if the Spanish monarchs would not give him boats in which to make his longed-for voyage.

II

The Spanish King was named Ferdinand, and the Spanish Queen was a beautiful woman named Isabella. When Columbus told them of his belief that the world was round, and of his desire to help the heathen who lived in this far-off country, they listened attentively to him, for both King Ferdinand and Queen Isabella were very earnest people and very desirous that all the world should become Christian, but their ministers and officers of state persuaded them that the whole thing was a foolish dream; and again Columbus was disappointed in his hope of getting help.

Still he did not give up in despair. *The thought was too great for that.* He sent his brother over to England to see if the English King would not listen to him and give the necessary help, but again he was doomed to disappointment. Only here and there could he find any one who believed that it was possible for him to sail round the earth and reach the land on the other side. Long years passed by. Columbus grew pale and thin with waiting and hoping, with planning and longing.

Sometimes, as he walked along the streets of the Spanish capital, people would point their fingers at him and say, "There goes the crazy old man who thinks the world is round." Again and again Columbus tried to persuade the Spanish King and Queen that if they would aid him, his discoveries would bring great honor and riches to their kingdom, and they would also help the world by spreading the knowledge of Christ and His religion. Nobody believed in him. Nobody was interested in his plan. He grew poorer and poorer.

At last he turned his back on the great Spanish court and, in silent despair, he took his little son by the hand and walked a long way to a small seaport called Palos, where there was a queer old convent, in which strangers were often entertained by the kind monks. Weary and footsore he reached the gate of the convent. Knocking upon it, he asked the porter, who answered the summons, if he would give little Diego a bit of bread and a drink of water. While the two tired travelers were resting, as the little boy ate his dry crust of bread, the prior of the convent, a man of thought and learning, whose name was Juan Perez, came by, and at once saw that these two were no common beggars. He invited them in and questioned Columbus closely about his past life.

He listened quietly and thoughtfully to Columbus and his plan of crossing the ocean and converting the heathen to Christianity.

Juan Perez had at one time been a very intimate friend of Queen Isabella; in fact, the priest to whom she told all her sorrows and troubles. After a long talk with Columbus, in which he was convinced that Columbus was right, he borrowed a mule and, getting on his back, rode for many miles across the open country to the palace at which the Queen was then staying. I do not know how he convinced her of the truth of Columbus' plan, when all the ministers and courtiers and statesmen about her considered it the foolish and silly dream of an old man; but somehow he did it.

He then returned on his mule to the old convent at Palos, and told Columbus to go back once more to the court of Spain and again petition the Queen to give him money with which to make his voyage of discovery. The State Treasurer said the Queen had no money to spare, but this noble-hearted woman, who now, for the first time, realized that it was a

grand and glorious thing to do, said she would give
her crown jewels for money with which to start
Columbus on his dangerous journey across the great
ocean.

This meant much in those days, as queens were
scarcely considered dignified if they did not wear
crowns of gold, inlaid with bright jewels, on all public occasions, but Queen Isabella cared far more to
send the gospel of Christ over to the heathen than
how she might look, or what other people might say
about her. With a glad heart Columbus hastened
back to the little town of Palos, where he had left his
young son with the kind priest, Juan Perez.

III

But now a new difficulty arose. Enough sailors
could not be found who would venture their lives by
going out on this unknown voyage with a crazy man
such as Columbus was thought to be. At last the
convicts from the prison were given liberty by the
Queen, on condition that they would go on with the
sailors and Columbus. So, you see, it was altogether
a very nice crew! Still, it was the best he could get,
and Columbus' heart was so filled with the great
work, that he was willing to undertake the voyage,

no matter how great or how many the difficulties might be. The ships were filled with food and other provisions for a long, long voyage.

Nobody knew how long it would be before the land on the other side could be reached, and many people thought there was no possible hope of its ever being found.

Early one summer morning, even before the sun had risen, Columbus bade farewell to the few friends who had gathered at the little seaport of Palos to say good-by to him. The ships spread their sails and started on the great untried voyage. There were three boats, none of which we would think, nowadays, was large enough or strong enough to dare venture out of sight and help of land and run the risk of encountering the storms of mid-ocean.

The names of the boats were the *Santa Maria,* which was the one that Columbus himself commanded, and two smaller boats, one named the *Pinta* and the other the *Niña*.

Strange, indeed, must the sailors have felt, as hour after hour they drifted out into the great unknown waters, which no man ever ventured into before. Soon all land faded from their sight, and on and on and on they went, not knowing where or how the voyage would end.

Columbus alone was filled with hope, feeling quite sure that in time he would reach the never-before-visited shores of the New World. On and on they sailed, day after day—far beyond the utmost point which sailors had ever before reached.

Many of the men were filled with a strange dread and begged and pleaded to return home. Still on and on they went, each day taking them farther and farther from all they had ever known or loved. Day after day passed, and week after week until two months had elapsed.

The provisions which they had brought with them were getting scarce. The men grew angry with Columbus and threatened to take his life if he did not command the ships to be turned back towards Spain, but his patience did not give out, nor was his faith one whit less. He cheered the hearts of the men as best he could.

He promised a rich reward to the first man who should discover the land. This somewhat renewed their courage; day and night watches were set and the western horizon before them was scanned at all hours. Time and again they thought they saw land ahead, only to find they had mistaken a cloud upon the horizon for the longed-for shore. Flocks of birds flying westward began to be seen. This gave some ground for hope. For surely the birds must be flying towards some land where they could find food, and trees in which to build their nests. Still, fear was great in the hearts of all, and Columbus knew that if land did not appear soon, his men would compel him to turn round whether he wished to or not.

Then he thought of all the heathen who had never heard of God's message of love to man through Christ, and he prayed almost incessantly that courage might be given him to go on. Hour after hour he looked across the blue water, day and night, longing for the sight of land.

At last one night, as he sat upon the deck of the ship, he was quite sure that a faint light glimmered for a few moments in the distant darkness ahead. Where there is a light there must be land, he thought; still he was not sure. So he called one of the more faithful sailors to him and asked him what he saw. The sailor exclaimed:

"A light, a light!"

Another sailor was called, but by this time the light had disappeared, so the sailor saw nothing, and Columbus' hopes again sank. About two o'clock that night the commander of one of the boats started to cry:

"Land, land ahead!"

You can well imagine how the shout was taken up, and how the sailors, one and all, rushed to the edge of their ships, leaning far over and straining their eyes for the hoped-for sight.

Early the next morning some of the sailors picked up a branch of a strange tree, lodged in the midst of which was a tiny bird's nest. This was sure evidence that they indeed were near land, for branches of trees do not grow in water.

Little by little the land came in sight. First it looked like a dim ghost of a shore, but gradually it grew distinct and clear. About noon the next day, the keel of Columbus' boat ground upon the sand of the newly discovered country.

At last, after a long life of working and studying, of hoping and planning, of trying and failing, and trying yet again, he had realized his dream.

The great mystery of the ocean was revealed, and Columbus had achieved a glory which would last as long as the world lasted. *He had given a new world to mankind!* He had reached the far-distant country across the ocean which scarcely any of his countrymen had ever believed to have any existence. He now *knew* that the whole round world could in time have the Christian religion.

He sprang upon the shore and, dropping to his knees, he first stooped and kissed the ground, and then he offered a fervent prayer of thanks to God.

A learned man who had come with him across the water next planted the flag of Spain upon the unknown land, and claimed the newly discovered country in the name of King Ferdinand and Queen Isabella.

Wonderful, wonderful indeed were the things which Columbus and the sailors now saw! Strange, naked men and women of a copper, or bronze color;

strange new birds with gorgeous tails that glittered like gems, such as they had never seen before; beautiful and unknown fruits and flowers met their gaze on every side.

The savages were kind and gentle and brought them food and water. Do you know, my dear children, that this strange, wild, savage country which Columbus had traveled so far and so long to discover was *our country? America?*

CHRISTOPHER COLUMBUS

With faith unshadowed by the night,
　Undazzled by the day,
With hope that plumed thee for the flight,
　And courage to assay,
God sent thee from the crowded ark,
　Christ-bearer, like the dove,
To find, o'er sundering waters dark,
　New lands for conquering love.

THREE OF OUR LORD'S MIRACLES

In order to convince the people that He was the Son of God, our Lord during His public life performed many miracles. Sometimes He raised the dead to life; at other times He cured the sick. He restored sight to the blind, hearing to the deaf, and speech to the dumb. In many other ways He used His almighty power to show that He was indeed the promised Redeemer of the world.

I. The Loaves and Fishes

One day, when He had retired with His disciples to a mountain, He was followed by a vast crowd of five thousand people. This was no accidental occurrence. In the designs of Providence it was brought about to furnish the occasion for His first lesson on the hard subject of the Holy Eucharist. It was a subject very dear to His Heart, and He was anxious to make it known. Here was a golden opportunity! The multitude, assembled from all parts of Judea for the Jewish Pasch, which was "near at hand," would as He knew, spread the news far and wide when they returned to their homes. Some of His miracles He wanted to be kept secret; but this one was to be published to the whole world.

Our Lord had it all planned, but He had not told any one about it, not even His Apostles. This may be gathered from the opening words of the Gospel which describe the memorable event. Calling Philip, who was one of the twelve, He asked, " 'Whence shall we buy bread that these may eat?' And this He said to try him, for He Himself knew what He would do." Our Lord may have hoped by this question to call forth from the Apostle some expression of faith regarding His power to feed the multitude miraculously. Philip, however, instead of exclaiming, "Lord, Thou canst do all things!" tried to figure it out mathematically, and answered helplessly, "Two hundred pennyworth of bread is not sufficient for them, that every one may take a little." How little can we do, when we trust only to human means, rather than to the power of God!

Then Andrew, another Apostle, the brother of Simon Peter, hoping to help matters along, remarked, "There is a boy here that hath five barley loaves and two fishes"; but added, "what are these among so many?" How cheerless they were! And

COPYRIGHT 1929 BY BENZIGER BROTHERS

all the while, our Lord, who was looking in vain for some expression of trust in Himself, was preparing for them a most unheard-of repast! His only answer to their hopeless replies was, "Make the men sit down." This done, He took the loaves from the fortunate little boy, "and when He had given thanks, He distributed to them that were sat down. In like manner, also of the fishes, as much as they would." When the people had eaten of the miraculous meal.

He directed the Apostles to gather up what was left; and lo! so bountifully had He provided for them, that twelve baskets were filled with the fragments that remained! On seeing the marvel, the people with one accord exclaimed, "This is of a truth the prophet that is to come into the world!" They had seen the miracles, and they believed! But, "blessed are they that have not seen and have believed."

II. The Marriage Feast

On another occasion He changed water into wine in answer to His Mother's wish. It was at a wedding feast, to which Jesus and Mary and some of the disciples were invited. The bride and bridegroom. who lived in a small town called Cana, were poor, so poor in fact that the wine they had provided was not sufficient for their guests. Before the end of the meal it gave out, a fact which Mary, because of her consideration for others, was quick to notice. Our Lord, who knew all things, must have been aware of it too; but for some reason He did not appear to know it, until His Mother, anxious to save the young couple from embarrassment, whispered to Him, "They have no wine." It was the work of a moment, a brief prayer, like the short aspirations indulgenced by the Church: but it touched the Heart of her Son and caused Him to work His first miracle. She made no request; she merely stated a fact. But no more was necessary when it was His Mother who prayed.

Now consider what followed this brief prayer. Jesus granted her request by changing water into wine! But His answer to her gentle appeal seemed at first like a refusal. It may even sound harsh to our ears, because we do not understand its spirit as she did. "Woman, what is it to Me and to thee? My hour is not yet come!" How should we have acted in Mary's place? How do we act when God seems to refuse what we ask?

Instead of taking this as a denial, Mary turned immediately to the waiters, and said quietly, "Whatsoever He shall say to you, do ye." She never for a moment doubted that He would do her will, even though His time for performing public miracles had not arrived. She understood too well the love and goodness of His Sacred Heart, and her own power over Him. How magnificently were her faith and trust rewarded! She had made no mistake, as none do who trust Him.

To the amazement of the waiters, He commanded that the water-pots be filled with water. What a

COPYRIGHT 1929 BY BENZIGER BROTHERS

strange order it must have seemed! But Mary had
told them to do whatsoever He should say; and lo!
when it was drawn out and brought to the chief
steward, it was no longer water, but sparkling wine!
In obedience to a mere suggestion from Mary, He
had performed a public miracle before His appointed time. Fortunate indeed were the bride and
bridegroom to have as their friend the Mother of
Jesus!

Now that she is in Heaven, her prayers are no less powerful. From her place beside her Divine Son, her slightest wish can still reach and move His loving Heart. Moreover, her anxiety for our welfare is as great as was her care for the young couple at the marriage feast. She is even more to us than she was to them; for she is our mother, given to us as such by our Lord as He hung upon the cross. Like a true mother, she is interested in all that concerns us, particularly in our eternal salvation. She who stood on Calvary, and saw the awful price of sin, knows the value of an immortal soul. She is tender and merciful to all who seek her protection. She will never fail those who invoke her with confidence. No sin is too great, no misery too deep, to win her help and compassion. Mary "conceived without sin" has been invoked by tempted souls, and they have triumphed over their temptations. She has been appealed to by souls steeped in the depths of shame and degradation, and they have had strength to leave their evil ways and rise to a new life of grace and virtue.

III. The Tempest

As might have been expected, those who saw our Lord's miracles were astonished, and at times terrified, at the power which could work such wonders. This was the case when He walked upon the waters.

After this, He preached in parables, the Parable of the Sower, of the Tares and the Wheat, of the Mustard-Seed and many another, wrapping up His teaching in a story which would bring the point home to His listeners. He spoke to the people in parables but, alone with His disciples, He explained all things to them.

Jesus had charged His disciples, while He preached by the waters of the great Galilean lake, that they should always have a boat in readiness for Him so that He could escape from the crowds when His preaching was done. Once they crossed the lake in a storm, and our Lord, tired out with preaching, fell asleep in the stern with His head upon a pillow. The wind blew and the water came into the ship so that it was sinking. Then they awoke Him, crying out: "Lord, save us: we perish." And He said to them: "Why are ye fearful? O ye of little faith!" He rebuked the waves and commanded them, saying: "Be still!" And the waves of the sea were still, knowing their King and Lord, and fawned on His boat in gentleness. And the storm died away. He stood there and the light flowed upon Him, and His face was like a light so that the disciples, in awe, dared not look at Him. Bending low in the boat, they whispered to each other: "Who is this, thinkest thou, that both the wind and the sea obey Him?"

APPLE BLOSSOMS

Have you plucked the apple blossoms in the spring?
    In the spring?
And caught their subtle odors in the spring?
    Pink buds pouting at the light,
    Crumpled petals baby white,
    Just to touch them a delight—
      In the spring.

Have you walked beneath the apple blossoms in the
    spring?
    In the spring?
Beneath the apple blossoms in the spring?
    When the pink cascades are falling,
    And the silver brooklets brawling,
    And the cuckoo bird soft calling
      In the spring.

If you have not, then you know not, in the spring,
    In the spring,
Half the color, beauty, wonder of the spring.
    No sweet sight can I remember,
    Half so precious, half so tender,
    As the apple blossoms render
      In the spring.

SONG OF SUMMER

Up in the tree-top, down in the ground,
High in the blue sky, far, all around,
Near by, and everywhere, creatures are living:
God in His bounty something is giving.

Up in the tree-top, down in the ground,
High in the blue sky, far, all around,
Near by, and everywhere, creatures are striving;
Labor is surely the price of their thriving.

Up in the tree-top, down in the ground,
High in the blue sky, far, all around,
Near by, and everywhere, singing and humming,
Busily, joyfully, summer is coming!

AUTUMN FIRES

In the other gardens
    And all up the vale,
From the autumn bonfires
    See the smoke trail!

Pleasant summer over
    And all the summer flowers,
The red fire blazes,
    The gray smoke towers.

Sing a song of seasons!
    Something bright in all!
Flowers in the summer,
    Fires in the fall!

31

THE WONDERFUL TAR BABY

For a long time Brer Fox had wanted to catch Brer Rabbit, but Brer Rabbit wouldn't be caught. At last, one fine day, Brer Fox had an idea. He got a chunk of tar and softened it with turpentine and made it into something that looked like a baby. Then he set this tar baby down by the side of the road and put a hat on its head and went away and hid in the bushes to see what would happen. He didn't have to wait long, for by and by Brer Rabbit came down the road—lippity-clippity, clippity-lippity, just as saucy as a jay bird. Brer Fox lay low. Brer Rabbit came along until he saw the tar baby; then he suddenly stood up on his hind legs as if he were astonished. The tar baby just sat there and said nothing. Brer Fox lay low.

"Good morning," said Brer Rabbit to the tar baby. "Fine weather this morning."

The tar baby didn't say a word. Brer Fox lay low.

"How do you think you feel this morning?" said Brer Rabbit to the tar baby.

Brer Fox in the bushes just winked his eye slowly and lay low; the tar baby didn't say anything.

"What's the matter with you? Are you deaf?" asked Brer Rabbit. "Because if you are, I can talk louder."

The tar baby kept still. Brer Fox lay low.

"You are stuck up. That's what you are!" said Brer Rabbit. "And I'm going to cure you of being stuck up. That's what I'm going to do."

Brer Fox chuckled softly, away down in his stomach. The tar baby said nothing.

"I'm going to teach you how to talk to respectable folks," said Brer Rabbit. "Take off that hat and say 'Good morning.'"

The tar baby kept still. Brer Fox lay low.

Brer Rabbit kept on talking to the tar baby, and the tar baby kept on saying nothing, until at last Brer Rabbit drew back and—blip! he hit the tar baby on the side of the head. And that's where he made a mistake, because his fist stuck fast to the tar baby. He couldn't pull it away. The tar held him. But the tar baby kept still and Brer Fox lay low.

"If you don't let me go, I'll hit you again," said Brer Rabbit; and with that—biff! he hit him with the other hand. That stuck fast, too. The tar baby said nothing. Brer Fox lay low.

"Let go, or I'll kick you!" said Brer Rabbit. The tar baby said nothing, but kept holding on tight. So Brer Rabbit kicked him with his right foot. That stuck fast, too.

"If I kick you with my other foot," shouted Brer Rabbit, "you'll think the lightning struck you."

The tar baby said nothing.

"Biff! he kicked the tar baby with his left foot; and his left foot stuck fast.

Then Brer Rabbit cried out that if the tar baby didn't let go, he would butt him in the stomach. So

he butted him in the stomach; and his head stuck fast.

Just then Brer Fox sauntered out of the bushes, looking as innocent as you please.

"Good morning, Brer Rabbit," said he, "you look a little stuck up this morning." Then he lay down and rolled on the ground, and laughed and laughed until he couldn't laugh any more. By and by he said:

"Well, I think I've got you this time, Brer Rabbit. Maybe not, but I think I have. You've been running around here and making fun of me for a long time, but I think you've got through now. You're always putting your nose into places where you have no business. Who asked you to come and get acquainted with that tar baby? And who got you so stuck up? You just jammed yourself up against that tar baby without waiting to be asked; and there you are, and there you'll stay until I gather up a brush pile and set fire to it; because I'm going to have you for dinner to-day."

Brer Rabbit was very humble. "I don't care what you do with me, Brer Fox," he said, "only don't throw me into that brier patch. Roast me if you must, Brer Fox, but don't throw me into that brier patch."

"It's so much trouble to kindle a fire, that I expect I'll have to hang you," said Brer Fox.

"Hang me as high as you please, Brer Fox," said Brer Rabbit, "but don't throw me into the brier patch."

"I haven't any string," said Brer Fox, "so I expect I'll have to drown you."

"Drown me as deep as you please, Brer Fox," said Brer Rabbit, "but don't throw me into that brier patch."

Now Brer Fox thought if Brer Rabbit didn't want to be thrown into the brier patch, that was the very

place where he should be. So he caught Brer Rabbit by the hind legs and threw him right into the middle of the brier patch. There was a great fluttering where Brer Rabbit struck the bushes, and Brer Fox waited to see what would happen.

By and by he heard something call, and away up the hill he saw Brer Rabbit, sitting cross-legged on a log, combing the tar out of his hair with a chip. Then Brer Fox knew he had been fooled.

Brer Rabbit shouted to him, "I was born and brought up in a brier patch, Brer Fox." And with that he skipped off, as lively as you please.

A TRAGIC STORY

There lived a sage in days of yore,
And he a handsome pigtail wore;
But wondered much, and sorrowed more,
   Because it hung behind him.

He mused upon this curious case,
And swore he'd change the pigtail's place,
And have it hanging at his face
   Not dangling there behind him.

Says he, "The mystery I've found,—
I'll turn me round,"—he turned him round;
   But still it hung behind him.

Then round and round, and out and in,
All day the puzzled sage did spin;
In vain—it mattered not a pin—
The pigtail hung behind him.

And right and left, and round about,
And up and down and in and out
He turned; but still the pigtail stout
Hung steadily behind him.

And though his efforts never slack,
And though he twist, and twirl, and tack,
Alas! still faithful to his back,
The pigtail hangs behind him.

A MAD TEA-PARTY

I. The March Hare and the Hatter

Alice was startled by seeing a large Cat, sitting on the bough of a tree, a few yards off. The Cat only grinned when it saw Alice. It looked good-natured, she thought, and so she spoke.

"Puss," she began, "would you tell me, please, which way I ought to go from here?"

"That depends a good deal on where you want to get to," said the Cat.

"I don't much care where—" said Alice.

"Then it doesn't matter which way you go," said the Cat.

"So long as I get somewhere," Alice added.

"Oh, you're sure to do that," said the Cat, "if you only walk long enough."

Alice tried another question. "What sort of people live about here?"

"In that direction," the Cat said, waving its right

paw around, "lives a Hatter; and in the other
direction lives a March Hare. Visit either you like.
They're both mad."

"But I don't want to go among mad people," said
Alice.

"Oh, you can't help that," said the Cat; "we're
all mad here. I'm mad. You're mad."

"How do you know I'm mad?" said Alice.

"You must be," said the Cat, "or you wouldn't
have come here." And with that he vanished.

Alice waited a little, half expecting to see him again, but he did not appear. After a minute or two she walked on in the direction in which the March Hare was said to live.

"I've seen hatters before," she said to herself. "The March Hare will be much the more interesting."

She had not gone very far before she came in sight of the house of the March Hare. She thought it must be the right house because the chimneys were shaped like ears, and the roof was thatched with fur.

There was a table set out under a tree in front of the house, and the March Hare and the Hatter were having tea. A Dormouse was sitting between them, fast asleep. The other two were using it as a cushion, resting their elbows on it, and talking over its head.

"Very uncomfortable for the Dormouse," thought Alice, "only as it's asleep, I suppose it doesn't mind."

The table was a large one, but the three were all crowded together at one corner of it. "No room! No room!" they cried out when they saw Alice coming.

"There's *plenty* of room!" said Alice, and she sat down in a large arm-chair at one end of the table.

"Have some jam," the March Hare said.

Alice looked all around the table, but there was nothing on it but tea. "I don't see any jam," she remarked.

"There isn't any," said the March Hare.

"Then it wasn't very civil of you to offer it," said Alice, angrily.

"It wasn't very civil of you to sit down without being invited," said the March Hare.

"I didn't know it was *your* table," said Alice; "it's laid for a great many more than three."

"Your hair needs cutting," said the Hatter.

He had been looking at Alice for some time with a great deal of curiosity, and this was his first speech.

"You should learn not to make personal remarks," said Alice; "it's very rude."

The Hatter opened his eyes very wide on hearing this, but all he *said* was, "Why is a raven like a writing desk?"

"Come, we shall have some fun now!" thought Alice. "I'm glad they've begun asking riddles. I believe I can guess that," she added aloud.

"Do you mean that you think you can find out the answer to it?" said the March Hare.

"Exactly so," said Alice.

"Then you should say what you mean," the March Hare went on.

"I do," Alice hastily replied; "at least I mean what I say—that's the same thing, you know."

"Not the same thing a bit," said the Hatter. "Why, you might just as well say that 'I see what I eat' is the same thing as 'I eat what I see'!"

"You might just as well say," added the March Hare, "that 'I like what I get' is the same thing as 'I get what I like'!"

"You might just as well say," added the Dormouse, who seemed to be talking in his sleep, "that 'I breathe when I sleep' is the same thing as 'I sleep when I breathe'!"

"It is the same thing with you," said the Hatter, and here the conversation dropped, and the party sat silent, while Alice thought over all she could remember about ravens and writing desks, which wasn't much.

The Hatter was the first to break the silence. "What day of the month is it?" he said, turning to Alice. He had taken his watch out of his pocket, and was looking at it uneasily, shaking it every now and then and holding it to his ear.

Alice thought a little and said, "The fourth."

"Two days wrong," sighed the Hatter. "I told

you butter wouldn't suit the works," he added, looking angrily at the March Hare.

"It was the *best* butter," the March Hare meekly replied.

"Yes, but some crumbs must have got in as well," the Hatter grumbled.

The March Hare took the watch and looked at it gloomily. Then he dipped it into his cup of tea and looked at it again, but he could think of nothing better to say than his first remark, "It was the *best* butter, you know."

Alice had been looking over his shoulder with some curiosity. "What a funny watch!" she remarked. "It tells the day of the month, and doesn't tell what o'clock it is."

"Why should it?" muttered the Hatter. "Does *your* watch tell what year it is?"

"Of course not," Alice replied very readily, "but that's because it stays the same year for such a long time together."

"Which is just the case with *mine,*" said the Hatter.

Alice felt dreadfully puzzled. The Hatter's remark seemed to her to have no sort of meaning in it, and yet it was certainly English.

"I don't quite understand you," she said.

"The Dormouse is asleep again," said the Hatter, and he poured a little hot tea on its nose.

The Dormouse shook its head and said, without opening its eyes,

"Of course, of course; just what I was going to remark myself."

"Have you guessed the riddle yet?" the Hatter said, turning to Alice again.

"No, I give it up," Alice replied; "what's the answer?"

"I haven't the slightest idea," said the Hatter.

"Nor *I*," said the March Hare.

Alice sighed wearily.

"I think you might do something better with the time," she said, "than wasting it in asking riddles that have no answers."

"If you knew time as well as I do," said the Hatter, "you wouldn't talk about wasting it. It's *him*."

"I don't know what you mean," said Alice.

"Of course you don't," the Hatter said. "I dare say you never spoke to Time!"

"Perhaps not," Alice cautiously replied; "but I know I have to beat time when I learn music."

"Ah! That accounts for it," said the Hatter. "He won't stand beating. Now, if you only kept on good terms with him, he'd do almost anything you liked with the clock. For instance, suppose it were nine o'clock in the morning, just time to begin lessons: you'd only have to whisper a hint to Time, and round goes the clock in a twinkling! Half-past one, time for dinner!''

("I only wish it was,'' the March Hare said to itself in a whisper.)

"That would be grand, certainly,'' said Alice thoughtfully: "but then—I shouldn't be hungry for it, you know.''

"Not at first perhaps,'' said the Hatter, "but you could keep it to half-past one as long as you liked.''

"Is that the way *you* manage?'' Alice asked.

The Hatter shook his head mournfully. "Not I,'' he replied. "We quarreled last March—it was at the great concert given by the Queen of Hearts, and I had to sing:

" 'Twinkle, twinkle, little bat!
How I wonder what you're at!'

You know the song perhaps?''

"I've heard something like it,'' said Alice.

"It goes on, you know,'' the Hatter continued, "in this way:

" 'Up above the world you fly,
Like a tea-tray in the sky.
            Twinkle, twinkle—!' "

Here the Dormouse shook itself, and began singing in its sleep, *"Twinkle, twinkle, twinkle, twinkle* ——" and went on so long that they had to pinch it to make it stop.

"Well, I'd hardly finished the first verse," said the Hatter, "when the Queen bawled out: 'He's murdering the time! Off with his head!' "

"How dreadfully savage!" exclaimed Alice.

"And ever since that," the Hatter went on in a mournful tone, "he won't do a thing I ask! It's always six o'clock now."

II. THE DORMOUSE TELLS A STORY

"Suppose we change the subject," the March Hare interrupted, yawning. "I'm getting tired of this. I vote the young lady tells us a story."

"I'm afraid I don't know one," said Alice.

"Then the Dormouse shall!" they both cried. "Wake up, Dormouse!" And they pinched it on both sides at once.

The Dormouse slowly opened its eyes.

"I wasn't asleep," it said in a hoarse, feeble voice, "I heard every word you fellows were saying."

"Tell us a story!" said the March Hare.

"Yes, please do!" pleaded Alice.

"And be quick about it," added the Hatter, "or you'll be asleep again before it's done."

"Once upon a time there were three little sisters," the Dormouse began, in a great hurry, "and their names were Elsie, Lacie, and Tillie, and they lived at the bottom of a well——"

"What did they live on?" said Alice, who always took a great interest in questions of eating and drinking.

"They lived on treacle," said the Dormouse, after thinking a minute or two.

"They couldn't have done that, you know," Alice gently remarked; "they'd have been ill."

"So they were," said the Dormouse, "*very* ill."

Alice tried a little to fancy to herself what such an extraordinary way of living would be like, but it puzzled her too much, so she went on, "But why did they live at the bottom of a well?"

"Take some more tea," the March Hare said to Alice, very earnestly.

"I've had nothing yet," Alice replied in an offended tone, "so I can't take more."

"You mean, you can't take *less*," said the Hatter; "it's very easy to take *more* than nothing."

"Nobody asked *your* opinion," said Alice.

"Who's making personal remarks now?" the Hatter asked.

Alice did not quite know what to say to this, so she helped herself to some tea and bread-and-butter, and then turned to the Dormouse and repeated her question: "Why did they live at the bottom of a well?"

The Dormouse again took a minute or two to think about it and then said, "It was a treacle-well."

"There's no such thing!" Alice was beginning very angrily; but the Hatter and the March Hare went "Sh! sh!" and the Dormouse sulkily remarked, "If you can't be civil, you'd better finish the story for yourself."

"No, please go on!" Alice said very humbly. "I won't interrupt you again. I dare say there may be *one.*"

"One, indeed!" said the Dormouse, indignantly. However, he went on. "And so these three little sisters—they were learning to draw, you know ——"

"What did they draw?" said Alice, quite forgetting her promise.

"Treacle," said the Dormouse, without considering at all this time.

Alice did not wish to offend the Dormouse again, so she began very cautiously: "But I don't understand. Where did they draw the treacle from?

"You can draw water out of a water-well," said the Hatter, "so I should think you could draw treacle out of a treacle-well—eh, stupid?"

"But they were *in* the well," Alice said to the Dormouse, not choosing to notice this last remark.

"Of course they were," said the Dormouse; "well in."

This answer so confused poor Alice that she let the Dormouse go on for some time without interrupting it.

"They were learning to draw," the Dormouse went on, yawning and rubbing its eyes, for it was getting very sleepy; "and they drew all manner of things—everything that begins with an M——"

"Why with an M?" said Alice.

"Why not?" said the March Hare.

Alice was silent.

The Dormouse had closed its eyes by this time, and was going off into a doze; but, on being pinched by the Hatter, it woke up again with a little shriek, and went on: "—that begins with an M, such as mouse-traps, and the moon, and memory, and muchness— you know you say things are 'much of a muchness'— did you ever see such a thing as a drawing of a muchness?"

"Really, now you ask me," said Alice, very much confused, "I don't think ——"

"Then you shouldn't talk," said the Hatter.

This piece of rudeness was more than Alice could bear; she got up in great disgust and walked off. The last time she saw them, they were trying to put the Dormouse into the teapot.

"At any rate I'll never go *there* again!" said Alice, as she picked her way through the wood. "It's the stupidest tea-party I ever was at in all my life!"

THE LITTLE POOR MAN

Seven hundred years ago, there lived in a little town of Italy, a boy, Francis Bernardone. The sun always shone on the little town of Assisi. Tall cypress trees hid the tiny stone houses. People loved flowers, and in every window you could see the colored blossoms, while at every square, peddlers sold the choicest of grapes and figs.

Francis loved the walled town of his birth. He never went far from home. Pietro Bernardone, the father of Francis, was a wealthy merchant. At the end of the day, little Francis and his good mother would wait at the gates of the city for the return of Pietro. Soon the shouting of the townsfolk, announcing the arrival of the wealthy merchant would be heard, then Pietro would be seen riding ahead followed by soldiers and pack horses loaded with rich cloth. A troop of soldiers protected the procession at the rear.

With the wealth of such a home, there was little in the mind of young Francis but the thought of how

lovely it was to be rich, to have everything he wanted, to be called the son of the richest merchant of Assisi. His playmates were the sons of royal families. The shouts and boasting of Francis often made his mother's heart ache.

"Francis has a good heart," she would say, adding, "God be good to my little boy."

The prayer of Francis' mother did make him an unusual boy. When the other boys bought sweets and toys, Francis would give his coins to a beggar.

"Foolish boy, Francis," said his companions.

"Are you trying to make a prince of that fellow?" asked others as they witnessed Francis clothing a poor man who passed the city gate.

Then came a great war. Francis had now grown to be a man. He had the heart of a soldier. He wanted to fight for the right. War to the heart of Francis was cruel. Victory with the enemy hurt and dying was not glorious to him. He was brave to the end of the war. He returned to Assisi, not the rich merchant's son, but a man with a bigger thought in his heart.

It was not long until the square that was once the scene of a rich home-coming of Pietro, now pictured a barefooted figure, dressed in a long brown tunic and girded with a heavy white cord about the waist. It was Francis who had heard the "call to arms" from the battleground of the Leader in the Heavenly Court.

Francis left his rich home. He soon forgot Assisi. He was never happier than when he helped to carry heavy stones with which to build a little country chapel. No one ever passed Francis without receiving some assistance. When he begged food, it was always shared with hungry children. Francis was richer and happier than he had ever been before.

Brother Francis soon had many followers. All

wore the long brown tunic and went barefooted. They
labored for all who were helpless and in need. The
"Little Army of Poor Men" was afterward known
as the Order of St. Francis.

THE SERMON OF ST. FRANCIS

Up soared the lark into the air,
A shaft of song, a wingéd prayer,
As if a soul released from pain
Were flying back to Heaven again.

St. Francis heard: it was to him
An emblem of the Seraphim:
The upward motion of the fire,
The light, the heat, the heart's desire.

Around Assisi's convent gate
The birds, God's poor who cannot wait,
From moor and mere and darksome wood
Come flocking for their dole of food.

"O brother birds," St. Francis said,
"Ye come to me and ask for bread,
But not with bread alone to-day
Shall ye be fed and sent away.

"Ye shall be fed, ye happy birds,
With manna of celestial words;
Not mine, though mine they seem to be,
Not mine, though they be spoken through me.

"Oh, doubly are ye bound to praise
The great Creator in your lays;
He giveth you your plumes of down,
Your crimson hoods, your cloaks of brown.

"He giveth you your wings to fly
And breathe a purer air on high,
And careth for you everywhere,
Who for yourselves so little care!"

With flutter of swift wings and songs
Together rose the feathered throngs,
And singing scattered far apart;
Deep peace was in St. Francis' heart.

He knew not if the brotherhood,
His homily had understood;
He only knew that to one ear
The meaning of his words was clear.

FRIENDSHIP

In long ago times, before our Lord was born, there lived in a heathen country two men who were friends. They loved each other as few brothers love. Their names were Damon and Pythias. The king of the country was Dionysius, and he was a tyrant of the worst type. Him Damon tried to kill; this was of course a wicked act; but Damon was a heathen and perhaps knew no better. Anyway, he was found out before he could do the deed, and the king ordered him to be crucified, and that was the worst and most ignominious death any one could possibly suffer. Damon was quite resigned; he only asked for three days' delay. For he had it in his power to restore his sister's husband to her family. The king consented on condition, as he mockingly said, he would find a hostage willing to die in his place should he not return. Damon went straight to his friend Pythias and explained the whole case to him. Without a moment's hesitation Pythias accepted the terms and bade his friend "God-speed."

Damon set out and accomplished his journey without any trouble. He left his sister happy with her newly restored husband, and began his return voyage.

But here trouble after trouble came upon him. Terrible rains fell and swamped the country. Rivers overflowed; bridges were swept away; no boats were to be had for love or money. At one stage of his journey Damon found his path flooded as by an angry sea. He stood on the banks and wept. It was twelve o'clock. If he had not reached his destination by nightfall, his friend would die in his place. The thought was agony. He sank on his knees and prayed to God, for though he was a pagan he believed in a Supreme Being.

Strengthened by his prayer, the poor traveler took heart and threw himself into the flood and struggled

with the rising waves as only a desperate man can. Dripping and exhausted, he reached the opposite side and made a dash for the town where his friend was preparing to die. There was no time for rest or refreshment, no time to think, only to act.

As he approached the place, he saw crowds gathering and he heard the remarks of the men hurrying by. "He is to die at sunset, to be crucified," they said. On and on went Damon. On the way he was met by a friend of his.

"Too late, Damon," he said. "Flee for your life. You cannot save your friend; at least save yourself."

Damon pushed him aside. "If I cannot save him, I will die with him," he cried.

The executioners were all ready; the beams were being fastened; the cords got ready. Pythias stood firm and undaunted. There was a movement in the dense mass of people, a swaying to and fro. Some one was approaching the king's chair of state. The guards would have kept off the intruder, but for his desperate violence. He reached the tyrant's chair and flung himself on his knees. Here he was, Damon, the condemned; let the king order the execution to be deferred. His friend must not die. Dionysius gave the order and asked what had happened. All was told to him: how Pythias had trusted his friend's

honor; how Damon had overcome almost insuperable
obstacles to be true to his trust, and how nobly both
had wished to die, the one for the other. The king
listened and was moved to pity. He forgave both
and, holding out his hands humbly, asked to be allowed to join the bond of friendship.

And I hope the two friends let him. Because I
think a noble friend is a thing a king may want and
not find.

THE STORY OF DANIEL

Six hundred years before the coming of our Savior, the great king of Babylon, Nebuchadnezzar, captured the city of Jerusalem. He carried away its king and many well-born young men who were forced to serve at his court. Among these youthful captives, four were Jews, Daniel and his three companions.

Whilst the other youths took part in the feasting and gayety at court, these four remained away. Because they were true to their religion, they refused to eat food which had been sacrificed to idols. The officer who was in charge of these young men feared that they would grow thin and pale and that he would be held responsible. But they asked to be fed on vegetables and plain water for ten days, as a test. At the end of their trial, they were healthier looking than ever, and so the officer let them keep to the plan. Instead of wasting their time in revelry, these four spent long hours in study and prayer. So they grew in the wisdom and power that comes from loving and serving God.

One night King Nebuchadnezzar dreamt a dream that puzzled him. When morning came, he sent for all his wise men to test them, ordering them to tell him what his dream had been and what it meant.

None of them could do as he commanded. They said it was not fair to expect them to tell him what he had dreamt but that if they knew his dream they could easily tell him its meaning. The King became very angry. He told them if they could not carry out his wishes, they would be cut in pieces, but if they did, they would be richly rewarded. Still the wise men persisted that they could not do this. They gave many reasons why they could not tell his dream. They said that no man on earth could do it.

Then the King became so greatly enraged that he commanded all the wise men of Babylon to be put to death.

However, when the soldiers of the King went to Daniel and his friends to kill them, Daniel told them that God had revealed the dream and its meaning to him, and that he would tell the King the things he wished to know.

And meanwhile Daniel had made this beautiful thanksgiving to God:

Blessed be the Name of God for ever and ever,
    For wisdom and might are His.
And He shifteth the times and the seasons;
    He removeth kings, and setteth kings aloft.
He addeth wisdom to the wise,
    And knowledge to them that already know,
He revealeth the deep and secret things,
    He knoweth what is in the darkness,
    And the light dwelleth with Him.
Thee I thank and Thee I praise
    O Thou God of my ancestors!
Who hast given me wisdom and strength,
    And hast made known to me
What we desired of Thee;
    For Thou hast made known to us
        The King's matter.

And Daniel, in chains, was led before the King. Nebuchadnezzar then asked him, "Well, what did I dream?"

Daniel answered, "Not by my own knowledge can I reveal to you your dream and its meaning, but only through God's help."

Then Daniel told the King his dream. The King, he said, had seen a great statue of metal, shining and beautiful. Its head was of gold, its breast and arms of silver, its waist and thighs of bronze, its legs of iron, and its feet of clay. And a great stone was cut out of the mountain-side, by no human hand, and it fell on the weak feet of the statue and crushed them, so that the whole figure crashed to the ground and was broken and crumbled into dust which the wind blew away. And the stone that shattered the statue grew and became a great mountain and filled the earth.

That was the dream.

This was what it meant.

The different parts of the statue were different empires. The golden head was Nebuchadnezzar, himself, and the empire of Babylon. The silver breast and the bronze waist were the empires of the Medes and the Persians. The iron legs represented the terrible march of Alexander who conquered all the Eastern empires. And the feet of clay meant Alexander's successors who, by dividing the empire, weakened the whole structure. And the great stone that fell so miraculously from the mountain-side meant the Kingdom of the Son of God that destroyed the old empires and then remained on earth to live and grow until it filled the whole world.

Strange to say, Nebuchadnezzar was much pleased with this answer. And he honored Daniel above all the great officers of Babylon.

LITTLE JESUS

Little Jesus, wast Thou shy
Once, and just so small as I?

And what did it feel like to be
Out of Heaven, and just like me?

Didst Thou sometimes think of there,
And ask where all the angels were?

I should think that I would cry
For my house all made of sky;

I would look about the air,
And wonder where my angels were;

And at waking 'twould distress me—
Not an angel there to dress me!

Hadst Thou ever any toys,
Like us little girls and boys?

And didst Thou play in Heaven with all
The angels that were not too tall?

Didst Thou kneel at night to pray,
And didst Thou join Thy hands this way?

And dost Thou like it best that we
Should join our hands to pray to Thee?

And did Thy Mother at the night
Kiss Thee and fold the clothes in right?

And didst Thou feel quite good in bed,
Kissed, and sweet, and Thy prayers said?

Thou canst not have forgotten all
That it feels like to be small.

And Thou knowest I cannot pray
To Thee in my father's way—

When Thou wast so little, say,
Couldst Thou talk Thy Father's way?

So, a little Child, come down
And hear a child's tongue like Thy own;

Take me by the hand and walk,
And listen to my baby talk.

To Thy Father show my prayer
(He will look, Thou art so fair)

And say: "O Father, I, Thy Son,
Bring the prayer of a little one";

And He will smile, that children's tongue
Has not changed since Thou wast young!

THE MAN OF THE HOUSE

Joseph, honored from sea to sea,
This is your name that pleases me,
     "Man of the House."

I see you rise at the dawn and light
The fire and blow till the flame is bright.

I see you take the pitcher and carry
The deep well-water for Jesus and Mary.

You knead the corn for the bread so fine,
Gather Them grapes from the hanging vine.

There are little feet that are soft and slow,
Follow you whithersoever you go.

There's a little face at your workshop door,
A little one sits down on your floor:

Holds His hands for the shavings curled,
The soft little hands that have made the world.

Mary calls you; the meal is ready:
You swing the Child to your shoulder steady.

I see your quiet smile as you sit
And watch the little Son thrive and eat.

The vine curls by the window space
The wings of angels cover the face.

Up in the rafters, polished and olden,
There's a Dove that broods, and his wings are golden.

You who kept Them through shine and storm,
A staff, a shelter kindly and warm.

Joseph, honored from sea to sea,
Guard me mine and my own roof-tree,
        "Man of the House"!

THE PINE-TREE SHILLINGS

"According to the most authentic records, my dear children," said Grandfather, "the chair, about this time, had the misfortune to break its leg. It was probably on account of this accident that it ceased to be the seat of the governors of Massachusetts; for, assuredly, it would have been ominous of evil to the commonwealth if the chair of state had tottered upon three legs. Being therefore sold at auction—alas! what a vicissitude for a chair that had figured in such high company!—our venerable friend was knocked down to a certain Captain John Hull. This old gentleman, on carefully examining the maimed chair, discovered that its broken leg might be clamped with iron and made as serviceable as ever."

"Here is the very leg that was broken!" exclaimed Charley, throwing himself down on the floor to look at it. "And here are the iron clamps. How well it was mended!"

When they had all sufficiently examined the broken leg, Grandfather told them a story about Captain John Hull and the Pine-Tree Shillings.

The Captain John Hull aforesaid was the mint-master of Massachusetts, and coined all the money that was made there. This was a new line of business; for, in the earlier days of the colony, the current coinage consisted of gold and silver money of England, Portugal and Spain. These coins being scarce, the people were often forced to barter commodities instead of selling them.

For instance, if a man wanted to buy a coat, he perhaps exchanged a bear-skin for it. If he wished for a barrel of molasses, he might purchase it with a pile of pine boards. Musket-bullets were used instead of farthings. The Indians had a sort of money, called wampum, which was made of clam-shells; and this strange sort of specie was likewise taken in payment of debts by the English settlers.

Bank-bills had never been heard of. There was not money enough of any kind, in many parts of the country, to pay the salaries of the ministers; so that they sometimes had to take quintals of fish, bushels of corn, or cords of wood, instead of silver or gold.

As the people grew more numerous, and their trade

one with another increased, the want of current
money was still more sensibly felt. To supply the
demand, the General Court passed a law for
establishing a coinage of shillings, sixpences and
threepences. Captain John Hull was appointed to
manufacture this money, and was to have about one
shilling out of every twenty to pay him for the
trouble of making them.

Hereupon all the old silver in the colony was
handed over to Captain John Hull. The battered
silver cans and tankards, I suppose, and silver
buckles, and broken spoons, and silver buttons of
worn-out coats, and silver hilts of swords that had
figured at court—all such curious old articles were
doubtless thrown into the melting-pot together. But
by far the greater part of the silver consisted of
bullion from the mines of South America, which the
English buccaneers—who were little better than
pirates—had taken from the Spaniards, and brought
to Massachusetts.

All this old and new silver being melted down and
coined, the result was an immense amount of splendid shillings, sixpences and threepences. Each shilling had the date, 1652, on the one side, and the figure
of a pine-tree on the other. Hence they were called
pine-tree shillings. And for every twenty shillings

that he coined, you will remember, Captain John Hull was entitled to put one shilling into his pocket.

The magistrates soon began to suspect that the mint-master would have the best of the bargain. They offered him a large sum of money if he would but give up that twentieth shilling which he was continually dropping into his own pocket. But Captain Hull declared himself perfectly satisfied with the shilling.

And well he might be; for so diligently did he labor, that, in a few years, his pockets, his money-bags, and his strong box were overflowing with pine-tree shillings. This was probably the case when he came into possession of Grandfather's chair; and as he had worked so hard at the mint, it was certainly proper that he should have a comfortable chair to rest himself in.

When the mint-master had grown very rich, a young man, Samuel Sewall by name, came courting his only daughter. His daughter—whose name I do not know, but we will call her Betsey—was a fine hearty damsel, by no means so slender as some young ladies of our own days. On the contrary, having always fed heartily on pumpkin-pies, doughnuts, Indian puddings, and other Puritan dainties, she was as round and plump as a pudding herself. With this round, rosy Miss Betsey did Samuel Sewall fall in love. As he was a young man of good character, industrious in his business, and a member of the church, the mint-master very readily gave his consent.

"Yes, you may take her," said he, in his rough way, "and you'll find her a heavy burden enough!"

On the wedding day, we may suppose that honest John Hull dressed himself in a plum-colored coat, all the buttons of which were made of pine-tree shillings.

The buttons of his waistcoat were sixpences; and the knees of his small-clothes were buttoned with silver threepences. Thus attired, he sat with great dignity in Grandfather's chair; and, being a portly old gentleman, he completely filled it from elbow to elbow. On the opposite side of the room, between her bridesmaids, sat Miss Betsey. She was blushing with all her might, and looked like a full-blown peony, or a great red apple.

There, too, was the bridegroom, dressed in a fine purple coat and gold-lace waistcoat, with as much other finery as the Puritan laws and customs would allow him to put on. His hair was cropped close to his head, because Governor Endicott had forbidden any man to wear it below the ears. But he was a very personable young man and so thought the brides-maids and Miss Betsey herself.

The mint-master also was pleased with his new son-in-law; especially as he had courted Miss Betsey out of pure love, and had said nothing at all about her portion.

So, when the marriage ceremony was over, Captain Hull whispered a word to two of his men-servants, who immediately went out, and soon returned, lugging in a large pair of scales. They were such a pair as wholesale merchants used for weighing bulky commodities; and quite a bulky commodity was now to be weighed in them.

"Daughter Betsey," said the mint-master, "get into one side of these scales."

Miss Betsey—or Mrs. Sewall, as we must now call her—did as she was bid, like a dutiful child, without any question of the why and wherefore. But what her father could mean, unless to make her husband pay for her by the pound (in which case she would have been a dear bargain), she had not the least idea.

"And now," said honest John Hull to the servants, "bring that box hither."

The box to which the mint-master pointed was a huge, square, iron-bound, oaken chest; it was big enough, my children, for all four of you to play at hide-and-seek in.

The servants tugged with might and main, but could not lift this enormous receptacle, and were finally obliged to drag it across the floor.

Captain Hull then took a key from his **girdle**, unlocked the chest, and lifted its ponderous lid. Behold! it was full to the brim with bright pine-tree shillings, fresh from the mint; and Samuel Sewall began to think that his father-in-law had got possession of all the money in the Massachusetts treasury.

But it was only the mint-master's honest share of the coinage.

Then the servants, at Captain Hull's command, heaped double handfuls of shillings into one side of the scales, while Betsey remained in the other. Jingle, jingle, went the shillings, as handful after handful was thrown in, till, plump and ponderous as she was, they fairly weighed the young lady from the floor.

"There, son Sewall!" cried the honest mint-master, resuming his seat in Grandfather's chair, "take these shillings for my daughter's portion. Use her kindly, and thank Heaven for her. It is not every wife that's worth her weight in silver!"

The children laughed heartily at this legend, and would hardly be convinced but that Grandfather had made it out of his own head. He assured them faithfully, however, that he had found it in the pages of a grave historian, and had merely tried to tell it in a somewhat funnier style.

As for Samuel Sewall, he afterwards became chief justice of Massachusetts.

"Well, Grandfather," remarked Clara, "if wedding portions nowadays were paid as Miss Betsey's was, young ladies would not pride themselves upon an airy figure, as many of them do."

THE BASQUE SONG

(The speaker is an old woman returning from church
after having received Holy Communion.)

O little lark, you need not fly
To seek your Master in the sky.
He's near our native sod.
  Why should you sing aloft, apart?
  Sing to the Heaven of my heart,
In me, in me, in me is God.

O travelers passing in your car,
Ye pity me, who come from far
On dusty feet, rough shod,
  You cannot guess, you cannot know,
  Upon what wings of joy I go
Who travel home with God.

Ships bring from far your curious ware.
Earth's richest morsels are your share,
And prize of gun and rod.
  At richer boards I take my seat,
  Have dainties angels may not eat.
In me, in me, in me is God.

O little lark, sing loud and long
To Him who gave you flight and song,
And me a heart of flame.
He loveth them of low degree,
And He hath magnifiéd me,
And Holy, Holy, Holy is His name.

WHAT I USED TO LOVE

I loved the Mother loved by Thee;
Saint Joseph, too, was friend to me,
How near Thy promised Heaven seemed to be,
  When shone, reflected in mine eyes
    The skies!

I loved to cull the grass, the flowers,
Forget-me-nots in leafy bowers;
I found the violets' perfume, all the hours,—
  With crocus growing 'neath my feet,—
    Most sweet.

I loved the daisies fair and white,
Our Sunday walks,—oh, what delight!
The azure skies so gloriously bright;
  The birds that sang upon the tree
    For me.

I loved my little shoe to grace,
Each Christmas in the chimney-place;
To find it there at morn how swift I'd race,
  The feast of Heaven, I hailed it well;
    Noel!

I loved my mother's gentle smile,
Her thoughtful glance that said the while:
"Eternity doth me from you beguile,
　　I go to Heaven, my God, to be
　　　　With Thee!"

I loved the swallows' graceful flight,
The turtledoves' low chant at night,
The pleasant sound of insects gay and bright,
　　The grassy vale where doth belong
　　　　Their song.

I loved to gather autumn leaves;
And where the moss a carpet weaves,
How oft among the vines, my hand receives
　　A butterfly, so light of wing,—
　　　　Fair thing!

I loved the glow-worm on the sod;
The countless stars so near to God!
But most I loved the beauteous moon, endowed
　　With shining disk of silver bright,
　　　　At night.

I loved upon the terrace fair
My father's reveries to share;
To feel his gentle kisses on my hair.
    I loved that father,—who shall tell
      How well?

We loved the sweet sound of the sea,
The storm, the calm, all things that be.
At eve, the nightingale sang from a tree;
    Oh, seemed to us like Seraphim
      Its hymn!

But came one day when his sweet eyes
Sought Jesus' cross with glad surprise . . .
And then—my precious, loving father dies!
    His last dear glance to me was given;
      Then—Heaven!

Now, Lord, I am Thy prisoner here;
Gone are the joys once held so dear,
I have found out,—none last, all seek their bier,
    I have seen all my joys pass by
      And die.

Jesus! Thou art the Lamb divine;
Naught else I crave if I am Thine,
In Thee all things in Heaven and earth are mine!
  Thou art the lovely Flower of Spring,
    My King!

In Thee I have the waving wheat,
The winds that murmur low and sweet,
All Mary's flowers, once blooming at my feet,
  The glowing plain, the tender grass I see
    In Thee.

The lovely lake, the valley fair
And lonely in the lambent air,
The ocean touched with silver everywhere,—
  In Thee their treasures all combined
    I find.

I have the barque on mighty seas,
Its shining track, the shore, the breeze,
The sun that sinks behind the leafy trees,
  Lighting the clouds, ere it expire,
    With fire.

In Thee the glorious stars are mine;
And often at the day's decline
I see, as through some veil silken and fine,
   Beckoning from Heaven, our fatherland,
     Thy hand!

O Thou who governest all the earth,
Who givest the mighty forests birth,
And at one glance makest all their life of worth!
   On me Thou gazest from above
     With love!

I hear, even I, Thy last and least,
The music from Thy heavenly feast;
There, there, receive me as Thy loving guest,
   There, to my harp, oh, bid me sing,
     My King.

Mary I got to see, and there
The saints, and those once treasured here;
Life is all past, and dried at last each tear,
   To me my home again is given,—
     In Heaven!

THE MINSTREL'S SONG

Once, long, long ago, there lived in a country over the sea a King called René, who married a lovely princess whose name was Imogen.

Imogen came across the seas to the King's beautiful country and all his people welcomed her with great joy because the King loved her.

"What can I do to please thee to-day?" the King asked her every morning; and one day the queen answered that she would like to hear all the minstrels in the King's country, for they were said to be the finest in the world.

As soon as the King heard this, he called his heralds and sent them everywhere through his land to sound heir trumpets and call aloud:

"Hear, ye minstrels! King René, our gracious King, bids you come to play at his court on May-day, for the love of Queen Imogen."

The minstrels were men who sang beautiful songs and played on harps; and long ago they went from place to place, from castle to castle, from palace to cot, and were always sure of a welcome wherever they roamed.

They could sing of the brave deeds that the knights had done, and of wars and battles, and could tell of the mighty hunters who hunted in the great forests; and of fairies and goblins, better than a story book; and because there were no story books in those days everybody, from little children to the King, was glad to see them come.

So when the minstrels heard the King's message, they made haste to the palace on May-day; and it so happened that some of them met on the way and decided to travel together.

One of these minstrels was a young man Harmonius; and while the others talked of the songs that they would sing, he gathered the wild flowers that grew by the roadside.

"I can sing of the drums and battles," said the oldest minstrel, whose hair was white and whose step was slow.

"I can sing of peace and joy," said the youngest minstrel, but Harmonius whispered: "Listen! listen!"

"Oh, we hear nothing but the wind in the tree-tops," said the others. "We have no time to stop and listen."

Then they hurried on and left Harmonius; and he stood under the trees and listened, for he heard something very sweet. At last he knew that it was the wind singing of its travels through the wide world; telling how it raced over the blue sea, tossing the waves and rocking the white ships, and hurried on to the hills, where the trees made harps of their branches, and then how it blew into the valleys, where all the flowers danced gayly in time to the tune.

Harmonius could understand every word:

"Nobody follows me where I go,
 Over the mountains or valleys below;
 Nobody sees where the wild winds blow,
 Only the Father in Heaven can know."

That was the chorus of the wind's song. Harmonius listened until he knew the whole song from beginning to end; and then he ran on and soon reached his friends, who were still talking of the grand sights they were to see.

"We shall see the King and speak to him," said the oldest minstrel.

"And his golden crown and the Queen's jewels," added the youngest; and Harmonius had no chance to tell of the wind's song, although he thought about it time and again.

Now their path led them through the wood; and as they talked, Harmonius said:

"Hush! listen!"

But the others answered:

"Oh! that is only the sound of the brook trickling over the stones. Let us make haste to the King's court."

But Harmonius stayed to hear the song that the brook was singing, of journeying through mosses and ferns and shady ways, and of tumbling over the rocks in shining waterfalls on its way to the sea.

"Rippling and bubbling through shade and sun,
 On into the beautiful sea I run;
 Singing forever, though none be near,
 For God in Heaven can always hear,"

sang the little brook. Harmonius listened until he

knew every word of the song and then he hurried on.

When he reached the others, he found them still talking of the King and Queen, so he could not tell them of the brook. As they talked he heard something again that was wonderfully sweet, and he cried: "Listen! listen!"

"Oh! that is only a bird!" the others replied. "Let us make haste to the King's court!"

But Harmonius would not go, for the bird sang so joyfully that Harmonius laughed aloud when he heard the song.

It was singing a song of green trees, and in every tree a nest, and in every nest eggs! Oh! the bird was so gay as it sang:

> "Merrily, merrily, listen to me,
> Flitting and flying from tree to tree,
> Nothing fear I, by land or sea,
> For God in Heaven is watching me."

"Thank you, little bird," said Harmonius, "you have taught me a song." And he made haste to join his comrades, for by this time they were near the palace.

When they had gone in, they received a hearty welcome, and were feasted in the great hall before they came before the King.

The King and Queen sat on their throne together. The King thought of the Queen and the minstrels; but the Queen thought of her old home, and of the butterflies she had chased when she was a little child.

One by one the minstrels played before them, the oldest minstrel sang of battles and drums just as he had said he would; and the youngest minstrel sang of peace and joy, which pleased the court very much.

Then came Harmonius. And when he touched his
harp and sang, the song sounded like the wind blowing, the sea roaring, and the trees creaking; then it
grew very soft, and sounded like a trickling brook
dripping on stones and running over little pebbles;
and while the King and Queen and all the court
listened in surprise, Harmonius' song grew sweeter,
sweeter, sweeter. It was as if you heard all the
birds in spring. And then the song was ended.

The Queen clapped her hands, and the ladies waved
their handkerchiefs, and the King came down from

his throne to ask Harmonius if he came from fairy-
land with such a wonderful song. But Harmonius
answered:

"Three singers sang along our way,
    And I learned the song from them to-day."

Now, all the other minstrels looked up in surprise
when Harmonius said this; and the oldest minstrel
said to the King: "Harmonius is dreaming. We
heard no music on our way to-day."

And the youngest minstrel said: "Harmonius is
surely mad! We met nobody on our way to-day."

But the Queen said: "That is an old, old song. I
heard it when I was a little child; and I can name the
singers three." And so she did. Can you?

THE LEGEND OF ST. CHRISTOPHER

For many a year Saint Christopher
   Served God in many a land;
And master painters drew his face,
   With loving heart and hand.
On altar fronts and churches' wall;
   And peasants used to say—
To look on good Saint Christopher
   Brought luck for all the day.

For many a year, in lowly hut,
   The giant dwelt content
Upon the bank, and back and forth
   Across the stream he went;
And on his giant shoulders bore
   All travelers who came,
By night, by day, or rich or poor,
   All in King Jesus' name.

But much he doubted if the King
  His work would note or know,
And often with a weary heart
  He waded to and fro.
One night, as wrapped in sleep he lay,
  He sudden heard a call—
"O Christopher, come, carry me!"
  He sprang, looked out, but all

Was dark and silent on the shore,
  "It must be that I dreamed,"
He said, and laid him down again;
  But instantly there seemed
Again the feeble, distant cry—
  "Oh, come and carry me!"
Again he sprang and looked; again
  No living thing could see.

The third time came the plaintive voice,
  Like infant's soft and weak;
With lantern strode the giant forth,
  More carefully to seek.
Down on the bank a little child
  He found—a piteous sight—
Who, weeping, earnestly implored
  To cross that very night.

With gruff good will he picked him up,
  And on his neck to ride
He tossed him, as men play with babes,
  And plunged into the tide.
But as the water closed around
  His knees, the infant's weight
Grew heavier and heavier
  Until it was too great.

The giant scarce could stand upright,
  His staff shook in his hand,
His mighty knees bent under him,
  He barely reached the land.
And staggering, set the infant down,
  And turned to scan his face;
When lo; he saw a halo bright
  Which lit up all the place.

Then Christopher fell down, afraid
  At marvel of the thing,
And dreamed not that it was the face
  Of Jesus Christ, his King.
Until the infant spoke, and said:
  "O Christopher, behold!
I am the Lord whom thou hast served,
  Rise up, be glad and bold!

"For I have seen, and noted well,
  Thy works of charity;
And that thou art My servant good
  A token thou shalt see.
Plant firmly here upon this bank
  Thy stalwart staff of pine,
And it shall blossom and bear fruit,
  This very hour, in sign."

Then vanishing, the Infant smiled,
  The giant left alone,
Saw on the bank, with luscious dates,
  His stout pine staff bent down.

I think the lesson is as good
  To-day as it was then—
As good to us called Christians
  As to the heathen men—

The lesson of Saint Christopher,
  Who spent his strength for others,
And saved his soul by working hard
  To help and save his brothers!

A CANOE TRIP DOWN THE
MISSISSIPPI

The English were not the only people that came across the ocean to live in America, for the French, too, thought it quite worth while to have colonies in the New World. The English made their settlements along the coast, but the French went farther inland and made settlements or built forts on the banks of the rivers. Only a few years after the English founded Jamestown, the French sailed up the Saint Lawrence River and founded Quebec.

Among the French colonists were fur-traders and Roman Catholic priests. Both were eager to push on into the wilderness far beyond the settlements. The traders wanted to buy furs of the Indians, and the priests wanted to tell the Indians about Jesus. Sometimes the Indians were friendly, but sometimes, when the hunting was poor, they said that the "Black-robes," as they called the priests, had brought sickness and famine upon them, and they tortured the earnest preachers or put them to death.

The traders and priests heard a great deal from the Indians about the country that lay beyond Quebec. One of their stories said that far, far to the west was a great river, whose name was Mississippi, or the father of waters.

When the Governor of Canada heard this, he was interested. Ever since the days of Columbus, two hundred years before, people had been hoping that some one would discover a channel across the great mass of land that is called America. They had learned that there was an ocean between America and Asia. Perhaps the Mississippi might flow into this ocean. The Governor decided to send Joliet, a fur-trader, and Father Marquette, a priest, to find the river and follow it till they could learn where it emptied.

So the priest and the trader, with five men to paddle, some smoked meat, and some Indian corn, set out in two birch-bark canoes. They paddled from the north end of Lake Michigan to Green Bay, and not far from there they came to the home of a tribe known as the Wild Rice Indians because they lived chiefly on wild rice. Father Marquette had preached to them before, and they were very glad to see him again. He told them that he had started to preach to distant tribes far away down the Mississippi.

"But, Father," they pleaded, "those tribes are

bad. They kill every stranger who comes among them."

"Our God will protect us against wicked men," replied Father Marquette.

"There is a frightful monster in the river," said the Indians. "You can hear it roar a long way off. It swallows up men and canoes. And high up on a rock demons live who will surely devour you. Father, do not go, we beg you."

"We will watch carefully," said the good Father, "and our God will help us, but we must go. I must tell the wicked tribes about Jesus. Now we will pray together before I start.'' So they prayed together and then said farewell. The little canoes floated away, and the Indians stood on the bank looking sadly after them.

Before long the voyagers caught sight through the trees of something white and shining. As they came nearer, they saw that it was a great white cross, and on it were hung deerskins, red belts, bows and arrows. ''What does this mean?'' asked the white men; and the Indians replied, ''A Blackrobe like this one,'' turning to Marquette, ''told us about the God of the Frenchmen. Last winter we were afraid of famine, but the good God sent us plenty of food, and we have put up the cross and hung our offerings upon it because we are grateful to him.''

With the help of these friendly Indians, they dragged their canoes to a stream that flowed into the Mississippi, and soon they were on the great river. Big, clumsy catfish bumped against their canoes. Other strange fish were caught, unlike any that the Frenchmen had ever seen before. They passed Indian villages, and at one of them they had a greeting that was a greeting indeed, for the chief declared that the earth was never so beautiful or the sun so bright as their coming had made it. The river was

never so free from rocks, and the corn was never so lovely. "I beg of you," he said earnestly, "do not go any farther down the river, for those bad Indians will surely kill you." "To lose my life for God's sake would make me very happy," said Marquette; and after a feast he and Joliet went to their canoes, the whole tribe going to the river-bank with them.

After a while the Frenchmen began to come to the dreadful things of which they had been warned. The "demons" were as harmless as kittens, for they were only two frightful pictures painted in red, green, and black, high up on a cliff. The "monster" was more of a danger, for its roaring proved to be the raging of the water among the rocks in a narrow channel. Much worse than monsters and demons was a tribe of Indians who gave them a great feast and then laid plans to kill them and steal everything that they had. They would have done this if their chief had not been on the watch, but he saw to it that the guests went safely on their way.

The Frenchmen had now been far enough to be sure that the river did not flow into the Pacific Ocean, but into the Gulf of Mexico. This was what the governor had sent them to find out. If they went farther among the savage tribes, they would probably be killed and all that they had learned would be lost. So they rested one day and then turned back.

There was no more of floating pleasantly down the river, for now they had to paddle upstream in the hot sunshine. It was a long, slow, tiresome journey of more than one thousand miles. Marquette stopped at Green Bay, and there he afterwards died. Joliet pushed on to Quebec to tell their story to the governor. Just before he came to Montreal, his canoe upset and his papers were lost. Marquette's were safe, and it is from these that this story of their journey is taken.

THE MASS

God made us; therefore, we belong to **Him**. As He does not wish us to forget that we are His, He commands us to worship Him alone. There is one act, and only one, by which we can pay Him the honor He deserves. This is the holy Sacrifice of the Mass.

A sacrifice is an offering made to God of something that is afterwards consumed. It is an act done to show God that we love and worship Him. Sacrifice has always been the greatest act of religion, and has been offered from the very beginning of the world. Before the coming of our Lord, the Jews offered animals and the first fruits of the earth. These were not worthy of God, but were pleasing to Him, because the time had not yet come to make known that there is only one Sacrifice by which He can be honored as He deserves.

When our Lord came, He taught many things that were not known before. Some of the greatest of these were made known at the very end of His life. At His death, the Old Law was to give place to the

New, that is, a better and higher form of religion was to be practiced. As there is no religion without sacrifice, this had to remain; but its form was changed. So great and holy was this change, that He chose one of the most solemn hours of His life in which to make it.

It was the night before He died. The Jews were celebrating a great holiday, which was known as the Pasch. According to the law, families gathered

together to eat of the Paschal lamb, with wild lettuce
and unleavened bread. Wine was also a part of the
feast.

All this had to be taken standing, and in the dress
of travelers. Psalms were sung, and the father of
the family related the history of the Jewish people.
After all this, the ordinary supper followed.

Our Lord, surrounded by His twelve Apostles, ob-
served the Pasch according to the law. It was the
eve of His death. In a few hours He was to begin
His passion. Before leaving the supper room to go
forth to suffer and die, He was to perform one of
the greatest acts of His life. He was to leave us His
greatest Gift. Above all, He was to make a change in
the kind of sacrifice by which God was to be wor-
shiped.

"Whilst they were at supper, Jesus took bread,
and blessed, and broke, and gave to His disciples,
and said, 'Take ye and eat. This is My Body.' And
taking the chalice, He gave thanks, and gave to them,
saying: 'Drink ye all of this. For this is My
Blood . . .' "

At first the Apostles did not fully understand our
Lord's meaning. Never before had He done anything so solemn, and it was some time before they
knew just what He meant. When our Lord said,

COPYRIGHT 1929 BY BENZIGER BROTHERS

"This is My Body," He meant that the bread was no longer bread, but had become, by His power, changed into His own Body. In the same way, the wine had been changed into His Blood. The Apostles could not see this change take place. What they saw *looked* like bread and wine. They knew, however, that our Lord spoke the truth, and that He wanted them to trust Him. They believed what He said, though they could not understand it. They

were the first to receive our Lord in Holy Communion, and they received It from His own hands.

But this was not all. Our Lord was about to leave them. He intended that all His children to the end of time should have the same happiness. He gave to the Apostles, therefore, the power to do as He had done, that is, to change bread and wine into His own Body and Blood. He had just said the first Mass; and He gave the Apostles a command that they should afterwards do as He had done. The sacrifices of the Old Law were at an end. The new Sacrifice was begun.

Ever since that time, the priests of the Catholic Church have obeyed this command of our Lord. Acting in His Name and by His power, they have offered to God the Body and Blood of His Son for the sins of the world. Our Lord offered Himself on the cross when He died on Good Friday; and the priests of the Church, who carry on the work of the Apostles, offer him each day in the Sacrifice of the Mass. We cannot fully understand this, any more than the Apostles could. But we can believe as they did, and adore our Lord, who can do all things. Through the Mass we can obtain all graces, and we can, moreover, offer to Him the one sacrifice that is worthy of His Holy Name.

THE LAMB

Little Lamb, who made thee?
Dost thou know who made thee?
Gave thee life and bade thee feed,
By the stream and o'er the mead?
Gave thee clothing of delight,
Softest clothing, woolly, bright,
Gave thee such a tender voice,
Making all the vales rejoice?
  Little Lamb, who made thee?
  Dost thou know who made thee?

Little Lamb, I'll tell thee;
Little Lamb, I'll tell thee;
He is calléd by thy name,
For He calls Himself a Lamb.
He is meek, and He is mild;
He became a little child.
I a child, and thou a Lamb,
We are calléd by His name.
  Little Lamb, God bless thee!
  Little Lamb, God bless thee!

CHILD'S EVENING HYMN

Now the day is over,
　Night is drawing nigh,
Shadows of the evening
　Steal across the sky.

Now the darkness gathers,
　Stars begin to peep.
Birds, and beasts, and flowers
　Soon will be asleep.

Jesu, give the weary
  Calm and sweet repose;
With thy tenderest blessing
  May mine eyelids close.

Grant to little children
  Visions bright of Thee;
Guard the sailors tossing
  On the deep blue sea.

Comfort every sufferer
  Watching late in pain;
Those who plan some evil,
  From their sin restrain.

Through the long night-watches
  May Thine angels spread
Their white wings above me,
  Watching round my bed.

When the morning wakes,
  Then may I arise,
Pure and fresh and sinless
  In Thy holy eyes.

THE STONE IN THE ROAD

There was once a very rich man who lived in a beautiful castle near a village. He loved the people who lived in the village and tried to help them. He planted trees near their houses, and made picnics for their children, and every Christmas he gave them a Christmas tree.

But the people did not love to work. They were very unhappy because they, too, were not rich like their friend in the castle.

One day this man got up very early in the morning and placed a large stone in the road that led past his home. Then he hid himself behind the hedge and waited to see what would happen.

By and by a poor man came along, driving a cow. He scolded because the stone lay in his path, but he walked around it and went on his way.

Then a farmer came, on his way to the mill. He complained because the stone was there, but he, too, drove around it and went on his way.

So the day passed. Every one who came by scolded because the stone lay in the road, but nobody touched it.

At last, just at night-fall, the miller's boy came past. He was a hard-working fellow, and was very tired, because he had been busy since early morning at the mill.

But he said to himself, "It is almost dark. Somebody may fall over this stone in the night and perhaps be badly hurt. I will move it out of the way."

So he tugged at the heavy stone. It was hard to move, but he pulled, and pushed, and lifted until at last he moved it from its place. To his surprise he found a bag lying beneath it.

He lifted the bag. It was heavy, for it was filled with gold. Upon it was written, "This gold belongs to the one who moves the stone."

The miller's boy went home with a happy heart, and the rich man went back to his castle. He was glad indeed that he had found some one who was not afraid to do hard things.*

* From *Studies in Reading* by Sears and Martin, published by The University Publishing Co.

MONI AND THE GOATS

Every family living in the little villages in the Alps mountains owns at least one goat. Boys are hired to take these goats up the mountains each morning, stay with them all day while they graze, and bring them back to their owners in the evening. Moni was one of the boys who did this work. The story you are about to read tells of something that happened one day to Moni's favorite goat.

In the sky the rosy morning clouds were disappearing and a cool mountain breeze rustled around Moni's ears, as he climbed with his goats for more than an hour, farther and farther up to the high cliffs above.

At last the height was reached where he usually stayed, and where he was going to remain for a while to-day. It was a little green table-land, with so broad a projection that one could see from the top all round about and far, far down into the valley. This projection was called the Pulpit-rock, and here Moni could often stay for hours at a time, gazing about

him and whistling away, while his little goats quite contentedly sought their feed around him.

As soon as Moni arrived, he took his provision bag from his back, laid it in a little hole in the ground, which he had dug out for this purpose, then went to the Pulpit-rock and threw himself on the grass in order to enjoy himself fully.

The sky had now become a deep blue; above were the high mountains with peaks towering to the sky and great ice-fields appearing, and far away down below, the green valley shone in the morning light. Moni lay there, looking about, singing and whistling.

The mountain wind cooled his warm face, and as soon as he stopped whistling, the birds piped all the more lustily and flew up into the blue sky. Moni was indescribably happy. From time to time Mäggerli came to Moni and rubbed her head around on his shoulder, as she always did out of sheer affection. Then she bleated quite fondly, went to Moni's other side and rubbed her head on the other shoulder. The other goats also, first one and then another, came to look at their keeper and each had her own way of paying the visit.

The brown one, his own goat, came very cautiously and looked at him to see if he was all right, then she would stand and gaze at him until he said: "Yes, yes, Braunli, it's all right, go and look for your fodder."

The young white one and Swallow, so called because she was so small and nimble and darted everywhere, like swallows into their holes, always rushed together upon Moni, so that they would have thrown him down, if he had not already been stretched out on the ground, and then they immediately darted off again.

The shiny Blackie, Mäggerli's mother, was a little proud; she came only to within a few steps of Moni, looked at him with her head lifted, as if she wouldn't appear too familiar, and then went her way again. The big Sultan, the billy-goat, never showed himself but once, then he pushed away all he found near Moni, and bleated several times as significantly as if he had information to give about the condition of the flock, whose leader he felt himself to be.

Little Mäggerli alone never allowed herself to be crowded away from her protector; if the billy-goat came and tried to push her aside, she crept so far under Moni's arm or head that the big Sultan no longer came near her, and so under Moni's protection the little kid was not the least bit afraid of him. Otherwise she would have trembled if he came near her.

Thus the sunny morning had passed; Moni had already taken his midday meal and now stood thinking as he leaned on his stick, which he often needed there, for it was very useful in climbing up and down. He was thinking whether he would go up to a new side of the rocks, for he wanted to go higher this afternoon with the goats, but the question was, to which side? He decided to take the left, for in that direction were the three Dragon-stones, around which grew such tender shrubs that it was a real feast for the goats.

The way was steep, and there were dangerous

places in the rugged wall of rock; but he knew a good path, and the goats were so sensible and did not easily go astray. He began to climb and all his goats gayly clambered after him, some in front, some behind him, little Mäggerli always quite close to him; occasionally he held her fast and pulled her along with him, when he came to a very steep place.

All went quite well and now they were at the top, and with high bounds the goats ran immediately to the green bushes, for they knew well the fine feed which they had often nibbled up here before.

"Be quiet! Be quiet!" commanded Moni; "don't push each other to the steep places, for in a moment one of you might go down and have your legs broken. Swallow! Swallow! What are you thinking of?" he called, full of excitement, for the nimble Swallow had climbed up to the high Dragon-stones and was now standing on the outermost edge of one of them and looking quite impertinently down on him. He climbed up quickly, for only a single step more and Swallow would be lying below at the foot of the precipice. Moni was very agile; in a few minutes he had climbed up on the crag, quickly seized Swallow by the leg, and pulled her down.

"Now come with me, you foolish little beast, you," scolded Moni, as he dragged Swallow along with him

to the others, and held her fast for a while, until she had taken a good bite of a shrub and thought no more of running away.

"Where is Mäggerli?" screamed Moni suddenly, as he noticed Blackie standing alone in a steep place, and not eating, but quietly looking around her. The little young kid was always near Moni, or running after its mother.

"What have you done with your little kid, Blackie?" he called in alarm and sprang towards the goat. She seemed quite strange, was not eating, but

stood still in the same spot and pricked up her ears
inquiringly. Moni placed himself beside her and
looked up and down. Now he heard a faint, pitiful
bleating; it was Mäggerli's voice, and it came from
below so plaintive and beseeching. Moni lay down
on the ground and leaned over. There below something was moving; now he saw quite plainly, far
down Mäggerli was hanging to the bough of a tree
which grew out of the rock, and was moaning piti-
fully; she must have fallen over.

Fortunately the bough had caught her, otherwise
she would have fallen into the ravine and met a sorry
death. Even now if she could no longer hold to the
bough, she would fall into the depths and be dashed
to pieces.

In the greatest anguish he called down: "Hold
fast, Mäggerli, hold fast to the bough! See, I am
coming to get you!" But how could he reach there?
The wall of rock was so steep here, Moni saw very
well that it would be impossible to go down that
way. But the little goat must be down there somewhere near the Rain-rock, the overhanging stone
under which good protection was to be found in rainy
weather; the goat-boys had always spent rainy days
there, therefore the stone had been called from old
times the Rain-rock. From there, Moni thought he

could climb across over the rocks and so bring back the little kid.

He quickly whistled the flock together and went with them down to the place from which he could reach the Rain-rock. There he left them to graze and went to the rock. Here he immediately saw, just a little bit above him, the bough of the tree, and the kid hanging to it. He saw very well that it would not be an easy task to climb up there and then down again with Mäggerli on his back, but there was no other way to rescue her. He also thought that if he asked the dear Lord to help him, he could not possibly fail. He folded his hands, looked up to Heaven and prayed: "Oh, dear Lord, help me, so that I can save Mäggerli!"

Then he was full of trust that all would go well, and bravely clambered up the rock until he reached the bough above. Here he clung fast with both feet, lifted the trembling, moaning little creature to his shoulders, and then climbed with great caution back down again. When he had the firm earth under his feet once more and had saved the terror-stricken kid, he was so glad he had to offer thanks aloud and cried up to Heaven:

"Oh, dear Lord, I thank Thee a thousand times for having helped us so well! Oh, we are both so

glad for it!" Then he sat down on the ground a
little while, and stroked the kid, for she was still
trembling in all her delicate limbs, and comforted her
for enduring so much suffering.

As it was soon time for departure, Moni placed
the little goat on his shoulders again, and said anx-
iously:

"Come, you poor Mäggerli, you are still trembling;
you cannot walk home to-day, I must carry you—"
and so he carried the little creature, clinging close to
him, all the way home.

TO MY LITTLE BROTHERS IN HEAVEN,
THY HOLY INNOCENTS

O happy little ones, with what sweet tenderness
   The King of Heaven
Blessed you, when here below! How often His caress
   To you was given!
You were the type of all the Innocents to come,
   In dreams I know
The boundless joy the King gives you in Heaven's
  high home,
   He loves you so!

It needs no precious stones, luminous and gay,
   To deck your hair;
The luster of your curls, sweet Innocents—to-day
   Makes Heaven more fair.
To you grand Martyrs lend their palms; they give
  their crowns
   Your brows to grace;
Upon their knees you find, dear children, now
  your thrones,
   In their embrace.

In splendid courts on high, with tiny cherub-throngs
  Gayly you play;
Beloved baby-band! your childish sports and song
  Charm Heaven alway!
God tells you how He makes the birds, the flowers,
  the snow,
   The sunlight clear:
No genius here below knows half the things
  you know,
   O children dear!

To Mary's welcoming arms, when your gay games
  are done,
   How swift you hie!
Hiding beneath her veil your heads like Christ her
  Son,
   In sleep you lie.
Heaven's darling little pets! audacity like this
   Delights our Lord!
And you can even dare caress and kiss
   His Face adored.

NO

I

"A, c-o-n con, Acon, c-a ca, Aconca —— oh, dear, what a hard word! Let me see—A-con-ca-gua. I never can pronounce it, I am sure. I wish they would not have such hard words in geography," said George Gould, quite out of patience. "Will you please tell me how to pronounce the name of this mountain, Father?"

"Why do you call this a hard word, George? I know much harder ones than that."

"Well, Father, this is the hardest word I ever saw," replied George. "I wish they had put the name into the volcano, and burnt it up."

"I know how to pronounce it," said Jane. "It is A-con-cagua!"

"A-con-cagua," said George, stopping at each syllable. "Well, it is not so very hard, after all; but I wish they would not have any long words, and then I could pronounce them easily enough."

"I do not think so," said his father. "Some of the hardest words I have ever seen are the shortest. I know one little word, with only two letters in it, that very few children, or men either, can always speak."

"Oh, I suppose it is some French or German word, isn't it, Father?"

"No, it is English, and you many think it strange, but it is just as hard to pronounce in one language as another."

"Only two letters! What can it be?" cried both the children.

"The hardest word," replied the father, "I have ever met with in any language—and I have learned several—is the little word of two letters, N-o, No."

"Now you are making fun of us!" cried the children; "that is one of the easiest words in the world." And to prove that their father was mistaken, they both repeated, "No, no, no," a great many times.

"I am not joking in the least," said their father. "I really think it is the hardest of all words. It may seem easy enough to you to-night, but perhaps you cannot pronounce it to-morrow."

"I can always say it; I know I can," said George, with much confidence. "No! Why, it is as easy to say it as to breathe."

"Well, George, I hope you will always find it as easy to pronounce as you think it is now, and be able to speak it when you ought to."

In the morning, George went bravely to school a little proud that he could pronounce so hard a word as "Aconcagua." Not far from the school-house was a large pond of very deep water, where the boys used to skate and slide when it was frozen over.

Now, the night before, Jack Frost had been changing the surface of the pond into hard clear ice, which the boys in the morning found as smooth as glass. The day was cold, and they thought that by noon the ice would be strong enough to bear.

II

As soon as the school was out, the boys all ran to the pond, some to try the ice, and others merely to see it.

"Come, George," said William Green, "now we will have a glorious time sliding." George hesitated, and said he did not believe it was strong enough, for it had been frozen over only one night.

"Oh, come on!" said the other boy; "I know it is strong enough. I have known it to freeze over in one night, many a time, so it would bear. Haven't you, John?"

"Yes," answered John Brown, "it did one night last winter, and it wasn't so cold as it was last night, either."

But George still hesitated, for his father had forbidden him to go on the ice without special permission.

"I know why George won't go," said John; "he's afraid he might fall and hurt himself."

"Or the ice might crack," said another.

"Perhaps his mother might not like it."

"He's a coward; that's the reason he won't come."

George could stand this no longer, for he was rather proud of his courage. "I am not afraid," said he; and he ran to the pond and was the first one on the ice. The boys enjoyed the sport very much, running and sliding, and trying to catch one another.

More boys kept coming on as they saw the sport, and all began to think there was no danger when suddenly there was a loud cry, "The ice has broken! the ice has broken!" And, sure enough, three of the boys had broken through and were struggling in the water. One of them was George.

The teacher had been attracted by the noise, and was coming to call the boys from the ice just as they broke through. He tore off some boards from a fence close by, and shoved them out on the ice until they came within reach of the boys in the water. After a while he succeeded in getting them out, but not until they were nearly frozen.

George's father and mother were very much frightened when he was brought home and they learned
how narrowly he had escaped drowning. But they
were so rejoiced to find that he was safe, that they
did not ask him how he came to go on the ice, until
after tea. When they were all gathered together
about the cheerful fire, his father asked how he came

to disobey his positive command. George said he did not want to go, but the boys made him.

"How did they make you? Did they take hold of you and drag you on?" asked his father.

"No," said George, "but they all wanted me to go."

"When they asked you, why didn't you say 'No'?"

"I was going to; but they called me a coward, and said I was afraid to go, and I couldn't stand that."

"And so," said his father, "you found it easier to disobey me, and run the risk of losing your life, than to say that little word you thought so easy to say last night. You could not say 'No'!"

George now began to see why this little word "No" was so hard to pronounce. It was not because it was so long, or composed of such difficult sounds; but because it often requires so much real courage to say it—to say "No" when one is tempted to do wrong.

Whenever, in after-life, George was tempted to do wrong, he remembered his narrow escape, and the importance of the little word "No." The oftener he said it, the easier it became; and in time he could say it, when needed, without much effort.

Boys and girls, whenever you are tempted to do wrong, never forget to say "No."

THE SUGAR-PLUM TREE

Have you ever heard of the Sugar-Plum Tree?
    'Tis a marvel of great renown!
It blooms on the shore of the Lollypop sea
    In the garden of Shut-Eye Town;
The fruit that it bears is so wondrously sweet
    (As those who have tasted it say)
That good little children have only to eat
    Of that fruit to be happy next day.

When you've got to the tree, you would have a hard
      time
   To capture the fruit which I sing;
The tree is so tall that no person could climb
   To the boughs where the sugar-plums swing!
But up in that tree sits a chocolate cat,
   And a gingerbread dog prowls below—
And this is the way you contrive to get at
   Those sugar-plums tempting you so.

You say but the word to that gingerbread dog
   And he barks with such terrible zest
That the chocolate cat is at once all agog,
   As her swelling proportions attest.
And the chocolate cat goes cavorting around
   From this heavy limb unto that,
And the sugar-plums tumble, of course to the ground,
   Hurrah for that chocolate cat!

There are marshmallows, gumdrops, and peppermint
      canes
   With stripings of scarlet or gold,
And you carry away of the treasure that rains,
   As much as your apron can hold!
So come, little child, cuddle closer to me
   In your dainty white night-cap and gown,
And I'll rock you away to that sugar-plum tree
   In the garden of Shut-Eye Town.

HIAWATHA'S CHILDHOOD

By the shores of Gitchee Gumee,
By the shining Big-Sea Water,
Stood the wigwam of Nokomis,
Daughter of the Moon, Nokomis.
Dark behind it rose the forest,
Rose the black and gloomy pine-trees,
Rose the firs with cones upon them;
Bright before it beat the water,
Beat the clear and sunny water,
Beat the shining Big-Sea-Water.

There the wrinkled, old Nokomis
Nursed the little Hiawatha,
Rocked him in his linden cradle,
Bedded soft in moss and rushes,
Safely bound with reindeer sinews;
Stilled his fretful wail by saying,
"Hush! the Naked Bear will get thee!"
Lulled him into slumber singing,
"Ewa-yea! my little owlet!
Who is this that lights the wigwam?
With his great eyes lights the wigwam?
Ewa-yea! my little owlet!"

Many things Nokomis taught him
Of the stars that shine in heaven;
Showed him Ishkoodah, the comet,
Ishkoodah, with fiery tresses;
Showed the Death-Dance of the spirits,
Warriors with their plumes and war-clubs,
Flaring far away to northward
In the frosty nights of Winter;
Showed the broad, white road to heaven,
Pathway of the ghosts, the shadows,
Running straight across the heavens,
Crowded with the ghosts, the shadows.

At the door, on summer evenings
Sat the little Hiawatha;
Heard the whispering of the pine-trees,
Heard the lapping of the water,
Sounds of music, words of wonder;
"Minnie-wawa!" said the pine-trees,
"Mudway-aushka!" said the water.
Saw the fire-fly, Wah-wah-taysee,
Flitting through the dusk of evening,
With the twinkle of its candle
Lighting up the brakes and bushes,
And he sang the song of children,
Sang the song Nokomis taught him:

"Wah-wah-taysee, little fire-fly,
Little, flitting, white-fire insect,
Little, dancing, white-fire creature,
Light me with your little candle,
Ere upon my bed I lay me,
Ere in sleep I close my eyelids!"

THE RACE

I

The twentieth of December came at last, bringing with it the perfection of winter weather. All over the level landscape lay the warm sunlight. It tried its power on lake, canal and river; but the ice flashed defiance and showed no sign of melting. The very weather-cocks stood still to enjoy the sight. This gave the windmills a holiday.

Nearly all the past week they had been whirling briskly; now, being rather out of breath, they rocked lazily in the clear, still air. Catch a windmill working when the weather-cocks have nothing to do!

There was an end to grinding, crushing and sawing for that day. It was a good thing for the millers near Broek. Long before noon they concluded to take in their sails, and go to the race. Everybody would be there—already the north side of the frozen Y was bordered with eager spectators; the news of the great skating match had traveled far and wide. Men, women, and children in holiday attire were flocking towards the spot. Some wore furs, and wintry cloaks or shawls; but many, consulting their feelings rather than the almanac, were dressed as for an October day.

The site selected for the race was a faultless plain of ice near Amsterdam, on that great arm of the Zuider Zee which Dutchmen of course must call—the Eye. The townspeople turned out in large numbers. Strangers in the city deemed it a fine chance to see what was to be seen. Many a peasant from the north-ward had wisely chosen the twentieth as the day for the next city-trading. It seemed that everybody, young and old, who had the wheels, skates or feet at command, had hastened to the scene.

There were the gentry in their coaches, dressed like Parisians, fresh from the Boulevards; girls from the orphan house, in sable gowns and white head-bands; boys from the Burgher Asylum, with their black pants and harlequin coats. There were old-fashioned gentlemen in cocked hats and velvet knee breeches; old-fashioned ladies, too, in stiff, quilted skirts and bodies of dazzling brocade. These were accompanied by servants bearing foot-stoves and cloaks. There were the peasant folk arrayed in every

possible Dutch costume—shy young rustics in brazen
buckles; simple village maidens concealing their
flaxen hair under fillets of gold; women whose long,
narrow aprons were stiff with embroidery; women
with short, cork-screw curls hanging over their foreheads; women with shaved heads and close-fitting
caps, and women in striped skirts and windmill bon-
nets. Men in leather, in homespun, in velvet and

broadcloth; burghers in model European attire, and burghers in short jackets, wide trousers and steeple-crowned hats.

There were beautiful Friesland girls in wooden shoes and coarse dresses, with solid gold crescents encircling their heads, finished at each temple with a golden rosette, and hung with lace a century old. Some wore necklaces, pendants and ear-rings of the purest gold. Many were content with gilt or even with brass, but it is not an uncommon thing for a Friesland woman to have all the family treasure in her head-gear. More than one rustic lass displayed the value of two thousand guilders upon her head that day.

Scattered throughout the crowd were peasants from the Island of Marken, with sabots, black stockings, and the widest of breeches; also women from Marken with short blue dresses, and black jackets, gaily figured in front. They wore red sleeves, white aprons, and a cap like a bishop's miter over their golden hair.

The children often were as quaint and odd-looking as their elders. In short, one-third of the crowd seemed to have stepped bodily from a collection of Dutch paintings.

Look at those boys and girls on stilts! That is

a good idea. They can see over the heads of the tallest. It is strange to see those little bodies high in the air, carried about on mysterious legs. They have such a resolute look on their round faces, what wonder that nervous old gentlemen, with tender feet, wince and tremble while the long-legged little monsters stride past them.

You know quite a number among the spectators. High up in yonder pavilion, erected upon the border of the ice, are some persons whom you have seen very lately. In the center is Madame van Gleck. It is her birthday, you remember; she has the post of honor. There is Mynheer van Gleck, whose meerschaum has not really grown fast to his lips—it only appears so. There are Grandfather and Grandmother whom you met at the St. Nicholas fête. All the children are with them. It is so mild they have brought even the baby. The poor little creature is swaddled very much after the manner of an Egyptian mummy, but it can crow with delight, and when the band is playing, open and shut its animated mittens in perfect time to the music.

Grandfather with his pipe and spectacles and fur-cap makes quite a picture as he holds Baby upon his knee. Perched high upon their canopied platforms, the party can see all that is going on. No wonder the

ladies look complacently at the glassy ice; with a
stove for a foot-stool one might sit cozily beside the
North Pole.

There is a gentleman with them who somewhat resembles St. Nicholas as he appeared to the young
Van Glecks on the fifth of December. But the saint
had a flowing white beard; and this face is as smooth
as a pippin. His saintship was larger around the
body, too, and (between ourselves) he had a pair of
thimbles in his mouth, which this gentleman certainly has not. It cannot be St. Nicholas after all.

Near by, in the next pavilion sit the Van Holps
with their son and daughter (the Van Gends) from
the Hague. Peter's sister is not one to forget her
promises. She has brought bouquets of exquisite
hot-house flowers for the winners.

These pavilions, and there are others beside, have
all been erected since daylight. That semi-circular
one, containing Mynheer Korbes' family, is very
pretty, and proves that the Hollanders are quite
skilled at tent-making, but I like the Van Glecks'
best—the center one—striped red and white, and
hung with evergreens.

The one with the blue flags contains the musicians.
Those pagoda-like affairs, decked with sea-shells
and streamers of every possible hue, are the judges'

stands, and those columns and flag-staffs upon the ice mark the limit of the race-course. The two white columns twined with green, connected at the top by that long, floating strip of drapery, form the starting point. Those flag-staffs half a mile off, stand at each end of the boundary line, cut sufficiently deep to be distinct to the skaters, though not enough so to trip them when they turn to come back to the starting point.

The air is so clear it seems scarcely possible that the columns and flag-staffs are so far apart. Of course the judges' stands are but little nearer together.

Half a mile on the ice, when the atmosphere is like this, is but a short distance after all, especially when fenced with a living chain of spectators.

II

The music has commenced. How melody seems to enjoy itself in the open air! The fiddles have forgotten their agony, and everything is harmonious. Until you look at the blue tent it seems that the music springs from the sunshine, it is so boundless, so joyous. Only when you see the staid-faced musicians you realize the truth.

Where are the racers? All assembled together

near the white columns.   It is a beautiful sight.
Forty boys and girls in picturesque attire darting
with electric swiftness in and out among each other,
or sailing in pairs and triplets, beckoning, chatting,
whispering in the fullness of youthful glee.

A few careful ones are soberly tightening their
straps; others halting on one leg, with flushed eager
faces suddenly cross the suspected skate over their
knee, give it an examining shake, and dart off again.
One and all are possessed with the spirit of motion.
They cannot stand still.   Their skates are a part of
them, and every runner seems bewitched.

Holland is the place for skaters after all.   Where
else can nearly every boy and girl perform feats on
the ice that would attract a crowd if seen in Central
Park?   Look at Ben!   I did not see him before.   He
is really astonishing the natives; no easy thing to
do in the Netherlands.   Save your strength, Ben,
you will need it soon.   Now other boys are trying!
Ben is surpassed already.   Such jumping, such pois-
ing, such spinning, such india-rubber exploits gen-
erally!   That boy with a red cap is the lion now;
his back is a watch-spring, his body is cork—no it is
iron, or it would snap at that!   He is a bird, a top,
a rabbit, a corkscrew, a sprite, a fish-ball all in an
instant.   When you think he's erect he is down; and

when you think he is down he is up. He drops his glove on the ice and turns a somersault as he picks it up. Without stopping, he snatches the cap from Jacob Poot's astonished head and claps it back again "hind side before." Lookers-on hurrah and laugh. Foolish boy! It is Arctic weather under your feet, but more than temperate overhead. Big drops already are rolling down your forehead. Superb skater, as you are, you may lose the race.

There are some familiar faces near the white columns. Lambert, Ludwig, Peter and Carl are all there, cool and in good skating order. Hans is not far off. Evidently he is going to join in the race, for his skates are on—the very pair that he sold for seven guilders! He had soon suspected that his fairy godmother was the mysterious "friend" who bought them. This settled, he had boldly charged her with the deed, and she, knowing well that all her little savings had been spent in the purchase, had not had the face to deny it. Through the fairy godmother, too, he had been rendered amply able to buy them back again. Therefore Hans is to be in the race. Carl is more indignant than ever about it, but as three other peasant boys have entered, Hans is not alone.

Twenty boys and twenty girls. The latter by this

time are standing in front, braced for the start, for
they are to have the first "run." Hilda, Rychie and
Katrinka are among them—two or three bend hastily
to give a last pull at their skate-straps. It is pretty
to see them stamp, to be sure that all is firm. Hilda
is speaking pleasantly to a graceful little creature in
a red jacket and a new brown dress. Why, it is
Gretel! What a difference those pretty shoes make,
and the skirt, and the new cap. Annie Bouman is
there too. Even Janzoon Kolp's sister has been admitted—but Janzoon himself has been voted out by
the directors, because he killed the stork, and only
last summer was caught in the act of robbing a bird's
nest, a legal offense in Holland.

This Janzoon Kolp, you see, was— There, I cannot
tell the story just now. The race is about to com-
mence.

Twenty girls are formed in a line. The music has
ceased. A man, whom we shall call the Crier, stands
between the columns and the first judges' stand. He
reads the rules in a loud voice:

"The girls and boys are to race in turn, until one
girl and one boy have beaten twice. They are to start
in a line from the united columns—skate to the
flag-staff line, turn, and then come back to the start-
ing-point; thus making a mile at each run."

A flag is waved from the judges' stand. Madame van Gleck rises in her pavilion. She leans forward with a white handkerchief in her hand. When she drops it, a bugler is to give the signal for them to start.

The handkerchief is fluttering to the ground. Hark!

They are off!

No. Back again. Their line was not true in passing the judges' stand.

The signal is repeated.

Off again. No mistake this time. Whew! how fast they go!

The multitude is quiet for an instant, absorbed in eager, breathless watching.

Cheers spring up along the line of spectators. Huzza! five girls are ahead. Who comes flying back from the boundary mark? We cannot tell. Something red, that is all. There is a blue spot flitting near it, and a dash of yellow nearer still. Spectators at this end of the line strain their eyes and wish they had taken their post nearer the flag-staff.

The wave of cheers is coming back again. Now we can see! Katrinka is ahead!

She passes the Van Holp pavilion. The next is Madame van Gleck's. That leaning figure gazing from it is a magnet. Hilda shoots past Katrinka, waving her hand to her mother as she passes. Two others are close now, whizzing on like arrows. What is that flash of red and gray? Hurrah, it is Gretel! She too waves her hand, but towards no gay pavilion. The crowd is cheering, but she hears only her father's voice, "Well done, little Gretel!" Soon Katrinka, with a quick merry laugh shoots past Hilda. The girl in yellow is gaining now. She passes them all, all except Gretel. The judges lean forward without seeming to lift their eyes from their watches. Cheer after cheer fills the air; the very columns seem rocking. Gretel has passed them. She has won.

"Gretel Brinker—one mile!"—shouts the crier.

The judges nod. They write something upon a tablet which each holds in his hand.

While the girls are resting—some crowding eagerly around our frightened little Gretel, some standing aside in high disdain—the boys form in a line.

III

Mynheer van Gleck drops the handkerchief this time. The buglers give a vigorous blast!

The boys have started.

Half way already! Did ever you see the like!

Three hundred legs flashing by in an instant. But

there are only twenty boys. No matter, there were
hundreds of legs I am sure! Where are they now!
There is such a noise one gets bewildered.

What are the people laughing at? Oh, at that fat
boy in the rear. See him go! See him! He'll be
down in an instant, no, he won't. I wonder if he
knows he is all alone; the other boys are nearly at
the boundary line. Yes, he knows it. He stops! He
wipes his hot face. He takes off his cap and looks

about him.   Better to give up with a good grace.   He
has made a hundred friends by that hearty, astonished laugh.   Good Jacob Poot!

The fine fellow is already among the spectators
gazing as eagerly as the rest.

A cloud of feathery ice flies from the heels of the
skaters as they "bring to" and turn at the flag-staffs.

Something black is coming now, one of the boys—
it is all we know.   He has touched the *vox humana*
stop of the crowd, it fairly roars.   Now they come
nearer—we can see the red cap.   There's Ben—
there's Peter—there's Hans!

Hans is ahead!   Young Madame van Gend almost
crushes the flowers in her hand; she had been quite
sure that Peter would be first.   Carl Schummel is
next, then Ben, and the youth with the red cap.   The
others are pressing close.   A tall figure darts from
among them.   He passes the red cap, he passes Ben,
then Carl.   Now it is an even race between him and
Hans.   Madame van Gend catches her breath.

It is Peter.   He is ahead!   Hans shoots past him.
Hilda's eyes fill with tears, Peter *must* beat.   Annie's
eyes flash proudly.   Gretel gazes with clasped hands
—four strokes more will take her brother to the
columns.

He is there!   Yes, but so was young Schummel just

a second before. At the last instant, Carl, gathering his powers, had whizzed between them and passed the goal.

"Carl Schummel, one mile!" shouts the crier.

IV

Soon Madame van Gleck rises again. The falling handkerchief starts the bugle; and the bugle, using its voice as a bow string, shoots off twenty girls like so many arrows.

It is a beautiful sight, but one has not long to look; before we can fairly distinguish them they are far in the distance. This time they are close upon one another; it is hard to say as they come speeding back from the flag-staff which will reach the columns first. There are new faces among the foremost—eager, glowing faces, unnoticed before. Katrinka is there, and Hilda, but Gretel and Rychie are in the rear. Gretel is wavering, but when Rychie passes her, she starts forward afresh. Now they are nearly beside Katrinka. Hilda is still in advance, she is almost "home." She has not faltered since that bugle note sent her flying; like an arrow still she is speeding towards the goal. Cheer after cheer rises in the air. Peter is silent but his eyes shine like stars. "Huzza! Huzza!"

The crier's voice is heard again.

"Hilda van Gleck, one mile!"

A loud murmur of approval runs through the crowd, catching the music in its course, till all seems one sound, with a glad rhythmic throbbing in its depths. When the flag waves all is still.

V

Once more the bugle blows a terrific blast. It sends off the boys like chaff before the wind—dark chaff I admit, and in big pieces.

It is whisked around at the flag-staff, driven faster yet by cheers and shouts along the line. We begin to see what is coming. There are three boys in advance this time, and all abreast. Hans, Peter and Lambert. Carl soon breaks the ranks, rushing through with a whiff! Fly, Hans; fly, Peter, don't let Carl beat again. Carl the bitter, Carl the insolent. Van Mounen is flagging, but you are strong as ever. Hans and Peter, Peter and Hans; which is foremost? We love them both. We scarcely care which is the fleeter.

Hilda, Annie and Gretel, seated upon the long crimson bench, can remain quiet no longer. They spring to their feet—so different, and yet one in eagerness. Hilda instantly reseats herself; none shall know how interested she is, none shall know how anxious, how filled with one hope. Shut your eyes then, Hilda—hide your face rippling with joy. Peter has beaten.

"Peter van Holp, one mile!" calls the crier.

VI

The same buzz of excitement as before, while the judges take notes, the same throbbing of music through the din—but something is different. A little crowd presses close about some object, near the column. Carl has fallen. He is not hurt though somewhat stunned. If he were less sullen he would find more sympathy in these warm young hearts. As it is they forget him as soon as he is fairly on his feet again.

The girls are to skate their third mile.

How resolute the little maidens look as they stand in line! Some are solemn with a sense of responsibility, some wear a smile half bashful, half provoked, but one air of determination pervades them all.

This third mile may decide the race. Still if neither Gretel nor Hilda win, there is yet a chance among the rest, for the Silver Skates.

Each girl feels sure that this time she will accomplish the distance in one half the time. How they stamp to try their runners, how nervously they

examine each strap—how erect they stand at last, every eye upon Madame van Gleck!

The bugle thrills through them again. With quivering eagerness they spring forward, bending, but in perfect balance. Each flashing stroke seems longer than the last.

Now they are skimming off in the distance.

Again the eager straining of eyes—again the shouts and cheering, again the thrill of excitement as, after a few moments, four or five, in advance of the rest, come speeding back, nearer, nearer to the white columns.

Who is first? Not Rychie, Katrinka, Annie nor Hilda, nor the girl in yellow—but Gretel—Gretel, the fleetest sprite of a girl that ever skated. She was but playing in the earlier race, now she is in earnest, or rather something within her has determined to win. That lithe little form makes no effort; but it cannot stop—not until the goal is passed!

In vain the crier lifts his voice—he cannot be heard He has no news to tell—it is already ringing through the crowd. *Gretel has won the Silver Skates!*

Like a bird she has flown over the ice, like a bird she looks about her in a timid, startled way. She longs to dart to the sheltered nook where her father and mother stand. But Hans is beside her—the girls are crowding round. Hilda's kind, joyous voice breathes in her ear. From that hour, none will despise her. Goose-girl or not, Gretel stands acknowledged Queen of the Skaters!

VII

With natural pride Hans turns to see if Peter van Holp is witnessing his sister's triumph. Peter is not looking towards them at all. He is kneeling, bending his troubled face low, and working hastily at his skate-strap. Hans is beside him at once.

"Are you in trouble, mynheer?"

"Ah, Hans! that you? Yes, my fun is over. I tried to tighten my strap—to make a new hole—and this botheration of a knife has cut it nearly in two."

"Mynheer," said Hansel, at the same time pulling off a skate—"you must use my strap!"

"Not I, indeed, Hans Brinker," cried Peter, looking up, "though I thank you warmly. Go to your post, my friend, the bugle will sound in a minute."

"Mynheer," pleaded Hans in a husky voice. "You have called me your friend. Take this strap—quick! There is not an instant to lose. I shall not skate this time—indeed I am out of practice. Mynheer, you must take it"—and Hans, blind and deaf to any remonstrance, slipped his strap into Peter's skate and implored him to put it on.

"Come, Peter!" cried Lambert, from the line, "we are waiting for you."

"For madame's sake," pleaded Hans, "be quick. She is motioning to you to join the racers. There, the skate is almost on; quick, Mynheer, fasten it. I could not possibly win. The race lies between Master Schummel and yourself."

"You are a noble fellow, Hans!" cried Peter, yielding at last. He sprang to his post just as the white handkerchief fell to the ground. The bugle sends forth its blast, loud, clear and ringing. Off go the boys.

See them, indeed! They are winged Mercuries, every one of them. What mad errand are they on? Ah, I know! they are hunting Peter van Holp. He is some fleet-footed runaway from Olympus. Mercury and his troop of winged cousins are in full chase. They will catch him! Now Carl is the runaway—the pursuit grows furious—Ben is foremost!

The chase turns in a cloud of mist. It is coming this way. Who is hunted now? Mercury himself. It is Peter, Peter van Holp; fly, Peter—Hans is watching you. He is sending all his fleetness, all his strength into your feet. Your mother and sister are pale with eagerness. Hilda is trembling and dare not look up. Fly, Peter! the crowd has not gone deranged, it is only cheering. The pursuers are close upon you! Touch the white column! It beckons—it is reeling before you—it—

Huzza! Huzza! Peter has won the Silver Skates!

"Peter van Holp!" shouted the crier. But who heard him? "Peter van Holp!" shouted a hundred voices, for he was the favorite boy of the place. Huzza! Huzza!

VIII

Now the music was resolved to be heard. It struck up a lively air, then a tremendous march. The spectators, thinking something new was about to happen, deigned to listen and to look.

The racers formed in a single file. Peter, being tallest, stood first. Gretel, the smallest of all, took her place at the end. Hans, who had borrowed a strap from the cake-boy, was near the head.

Three gaily twined arches were placed at intervals upon the river facing the Van Gleck pavilion.

Skating slowly, and in perfect time to the music, the boys and girls moved forward, led on by Peter. It was beautiful to see the bright procession glide along like a living creature. It curved and doubled, and drew its graceful length in and out among the arches—whichever way Peter the head went, the body was sure to follow. Sometimes it steered direct for the center arch, then, as if seized with a new impulse, turned away and curled itself about the first one; then unwound slowly and bending low, with quick, snakelike curvings, crossed the river, passing at length through the farthest arch.

When the music was slow, the procession seemed to crawl like a thing afraid; it grew livelier, and the creature darted forward with a spring, gliding rapidly among the arches, in and out, curling, twisting, turning, never losing form until, at the shrill call of the bugle rising above the music, it suddenly resolved itself into boys and girls standing in double semi-circle before Madame van Gleck's pavilion.

Peter and Gretel stand in the center in advance of the others. Madame van Gleck rises majestically, Gretel trembles, but feels that she must look at the beautiful lady. She cannot hear what is said, there is such a buzzing all around her. She is thinking that she ought to try and make a curtsy, such as her mother makes to the meester, when suddenly something so dazzling is placed in her hand that she gives a cry of joy.

Then she ventures to look about her. Peter, too, has something in his hands— "Oh! oh! how splendid!" she cries, and "Oh! how splendid!" is echoed as far as people can see.

Meantime the silver skates flash in the sunshine, throwing dashes of light upon those two happy faces.

Mevrouw van Gend sends a little messenger with her bouquets. One for Hilda, one for Carl, and others for Peter and Gretel.

At sight of the flowers the Queen of the Skaters becomes uncontrollable. With a bright stare of gratitude she gathers skates and bouquet in her apron— hugs them to her bosom, and darts off to search for her father and mother in the scattering crowd.

NO BOY KNOWS

There are many things that boys may know—
Why this and that are thus and so,
Who made the world in the dark and lit
The great sun up to lighten it;
Boys know new things every day—
When they study, or when they play,
When they idle, or sow or reap—
But no boy knows when he goes to sleep.

Boys who listen—or should at least—
May know that the round old earth rolls east,
And know that the ice and the snow and the rain—
Ever repeating their parts again—
Are all just water, and the sunbeams first
Sip from the earth in their endless thirst,
And pour again till the low streams leap—
But no boy knows when he goes to sleep.

A boy may know what a long glad while
It has been to him since the dawn's first smile,
When forth he fared in the realm divine
Of brook-laced woodland and spun-sunshine;
He may know each call of his truant mates,
And the paths they went—and the pasture gates
Of the 'cross-lots home through the dusk so deep—
But no boy knows when he goes to sleep.

Oh, I have followed me, o'er and o'er,
From the fragrant drowse on the parlor floor
To the pleading voice of the mother when
I even doubted I heard it then—
To the sense of a kiss, and a moonlit room,
And dewy odors of locust bloom—
A sweet white cot—and a cricket's cheep—
But no boy knows when he goes to sleep.*

* By James Whitcomb Riley, from *The Book of Joyous Children*, copyright 1902, used by special permission of the publishers, The Bobbs-Merrill Company.

FIRST RAIN

When Eve walked in her garden
  With Adam by her side,
And God was still the warden,
  And she was still a bride,
How great was her amazement
  To see when twilight died,
The first moon at the casement
  Of evening, open wide!

But greater than her wonder
  At star, or bird, or tree,
Or afterward at thunder,
  Or delicate deer or bee,
Was her flushed awe one morning,
  When down the clouded air
With freshened winds for warning,
  Came water,—everywhere!

NAHUM PRINCE

This is the story of Nahum Prince. He must have lived a hundred years or more ago, and he died, I do not know when. He was lame. Something had crushed his foot so that he could hardly walk.

It was at the time of the fighting with Burgoyne, and General Lincoln was in front and was ordering out every man from New Hampshire. And all the regular companies of troops had been marched out. Then there came the final call for all who could go, and all the old men and boys volunteered; and there was not a boy over thirteen years of age in the village that didn't go, except Nahum Prince. When they were getting ready to go, he stood up as well as he could with an old Queen Anne's arm on his shoulder. And the captain came along and saw him and said:

"Nahum, you here!"

"Yes, sir," said Nahum.

Then the captain said: "Go home, Nahum; you know you don't belong here; you can't walk a mile."

Then he called to the doctor, and the doctor said, "Nahum, it's no use; you must go home."

Then they all marched off without him.

172

Rub-a-dub-dub; rub-a-dub-dub, went the drums; and every man and boy of them went off and left poor Nahum Prince alone. He had a good home, but he was very homesick all that night and didn't sleep much; and the next morning he said:

"I shall die before night if I stay here all alone, the only boy in town. I must do something."

It was coming autumn. It was not late, but he knew he must do something; so he went down and split old Widow Corliss' wood for her, for he could split wood though he could not march.

He had not been splitting wood for more than an hour when four men on horseback came down the road and stopped. He could see them stand and talk. They all went off and then came back again and beckoned to Nahum; and when he came up, the man on horseback said,

"Where are all the men gone?"

"They have all gone off to join the army," Nahum said.

"And isn't there any blacksmith in town?"

"No," said Nahum, "there isn't a man or a boy in the town except me, and I wouldn't be here only I am so lame I can't march."

"Do you mean to tell me," said the man, "that there is nobody here who can set a shoe?"

"Why, I can set a shoe," said Nahum.

"Then it is lucky you are left behind," the man said. "Light up the forge and set this shoe."

And now comes the most interesting part of the story. Nahum lighted the fire, blew the flames hot, and set the shoe on the horse; and the horse and the rider went away after the man had thanked Nahum.

Nahum finished splitting the widow's wood. And when, the next week, the boys came home and told how Colonel Seth Warner came up on his horse just in time, leading the First Regiment, and took the prisoners and won the day, Nahum didn't say anything. But he knew that Colonel Warner never would have been on that horse if he hadn't set that shoe. And it was little lame Nahum Prince who really won the splendid victory which ended the battle of Bennington.

BIRD HABITS

HIS TRAVELS

Most of our birds take two long journeys every year, one in the fall to the South and the other in the spring back to the North. These journeys are called "Migrations."

The birds do not go all at once, but in many cases those of a kind who live near each other collect in a flock and travel together. Each species or kind has its own time to go.

It may be thought that it is because of the cold that so many birds move to a warmer climate. But it is not so; they are very well dressed to endure cold. Their feather suits are so warm that some of our smallest and weakest birds are able to stay with us, like the chickadee, and the golden-crowned kinglet. It is simply because they cannot get food in winter, that they have to go.

The fall travel begins soon after the first of July.

The bobolink is one of the first to leave us; though he does not start at once on his long journey. By that time his little folk are full grown, and can take care of themselves, and he is getting on his winter suit, or moulting.

Then some morning all the bobolinks in the country are turned out of their homes in the meadows by men and horses and mowing machines, for at that time the long grass is ready to cut.

Then he begins to think about the wild rice that is getting just right to eat. Besides, he likes to take his long journey to South America in an easy way, stopping here and there as he goes. So some morning we miss his cheerful call, and if we go to the meadow we shall not be able to see a single bobolink.

There, too, are the swallows, who eat only small flying insects. As the weather grows cooler, these tiny flies are no longer to be found. So the swallows begin to flock, as it is called. For a few days they will be seen on fences and telegraph wires, chattering and making a great noise, and then some morning they will all be gone.

They spend some time in marshes and lonely places before they at last set out for the South.

As the days grow shorter and cooler, the warblers go. These are the bright-colored little fellows, who

live mostly in the tops of trees. Then the orioles and
the thrushes and the cuckoos leave us, and most birds
who live on insects.

By the time that November comes in, few of them
will be left. Birds who can live on seeds and winter
berries, such as cedar berries and partridge-berries,
and others, often stay with us—bluebirds, finches,
and sometimes robins.

Many birds take their journeys by night. Think
of it! Tiny creatures that all summer go to bed by
dark, start off some night, when it seems as if they
ought to be asleep, and fly all night in the dark.

When it grows light, they stop in some place where
they can feed and rest. And the next night, or two
or three nights later, they go on again. So they do
until they reach their winter homes, hundreds or
thousands of miles away.

These night flyers are the timid birds, and those
who live in the woods and do not like to be seen—
thrushes, wrens, vireos and others. Birds with strong
wings, who are used to flying hours every day, and
bolder birds, who do not mind being seen, take their
journeys by daylight.

Most of them stop now and then, a day or two at a
time, to feed and rest. They fly very high and faster
than our railroad trains can go.

In the spring the birds take their second long journey, back to their last year's home.

How they know their way on those journeys, men have been for many years trying to find out. They have found that birds travel on regular roads, or routes, that follow the rivers and the shore of the ocean. They can see much better than we can, and even in the night they can see water.

One such road, or highway, is over the harbor of New York. When the Statue of Liberty was set up on an island in the harbor, it was put in the bird's path.

Usually they fly too high to mind it; but when there is a rain or fog they come much lower, and, sad to say, many of them fly against it and are killed.

We often see strange birds in our city streets and parks, while they are passing through on their migration, for they sometimes spend several days with us.

GAY ROBIN

Gay Robin is seen no more:
 He is gone with the snow,
 For winter is o'er
 And Robin will go.

In need he was fed, and now he has fled,
    Away to his secret nest.
    No more will he stand
    Begging crumbs,
    No longer he comes
    Beseeching our hand
    And showing his breast
    At window and door;
Gay Robin is seen no more.

Blithe Robin is heard no more;
    He gave us his song
    When summer was o'er
    And winter was long:
He sang for his bread and now he has fled
    Away to his secret nest.
    And there in the green
    Early and late
    Alone to his mate
    He pipeth unseen
    And swelleth his breast.
    For us it is o'er,
Blithe Robin is heard no more.

A CHILD'S EVENSONG

The sun is weary, for he ran
  So far and fast to-day;
The birds are weary, for who sang
  So many songs as they?
The bees and butterflies at last
  Are tired out, for just think too
How many gardens through the day
  Their little wings have fluttered through.
  And so, as all tired people do,
They've gone to lay their sleepy heads
Deep, deep in warm and happy beds.
The sun has shut his golden eye,
And gone to sleep beneath the sky,
The birds and butterflies and bees
Have all crept into flowers and trees,
And all lie quiet, still as mice,
Till morning comes—like father's voice.

So Geoffrey, Owen, Phyllis, you
Must sleep away till morning too.
Close little eyes, down little heads,
And sleep—sleep—sleep in happy beds.

THE CHILDREN'S HOUR

Between the dark and the daylight,
  When the night is beginning to lower,
Comes a pause in the day's occupations,
  That is known as the Children's Hour.

I hear in the chamber above me
  The patter of little feet,
The sound of a door that is opened,
  And voices soft and sweet.

From my study I see in the lamplight,
  Descending the broad hall stair,
Grave Alice, and laughing Allegra,
  And Edith with golden hair.

A whisper, and then a silence:
  Yet I know by their merry eyes
They are plotting and planning together
  To take me by surprise.

A sudden rush from the stairway,
  A sudden raid from the hall!
By three doors left unguarded
  They enter my castle wall!

They climb up into my turret
  O'er the arms and back of my chair;
If I try to escape, they surround me;
  They seem to be everywhere.

They almost devour me with kisses,
  Their arms about me entwine,
Till I think of the Bishop of Bingen
  In his Mouse-Tower on the Rhine!

Do you think, O blue-eyed banditti,
  Because you have scaled the wall,
Such an old mustache as I am
  Is not a match for you all!

I have you fast in my fortress,
  And will not let you depart,
But put you down into the dungeon
  In the round-tower of my heart.

And there will I keep you forever,
  Yes, forever and a day,
Till the walls shall crumble to ruin,
  And moulder in dust away!

LITTLE SAN PETER

"When we first came into this part of the country," said the gray-haired mother, "there were only bands of Indians, with occasionally a French fur-trader living among them. Usually these traders had Indian wives. As our settlement began to develop, and we established our schools, some of these traders, thinking of their old life before they joined the Indians, desired to have their children taught the ways of the Whites.

"One day old Bruere with his Sioux wife and his three children came to our house and made a rather strange request of my father and mother. He wanted him to take his three French-Indian children, Roxie, Marie, and Little St. Pierre, and board them through the winter while they went with us children to the village school.

"Father hesitated, but Bruere pressed his request, saying he would bring buckskin, clothing, buffalo robes, and game to clothe and feed not only his own children, but also to help our family. We were having no easy time of it to get along. This looked like an opportunity both to add things of comfort and to bring joy and uplift to these children of the tepee; so Mother decided the question by saying that she was willing to add the children to her family and do her best by them.

"Autumn went by happily and winter wore along fairly well until February came. Then the snow fell so deep it nearly buried our log cabin. We could not get out for a time even for school. The cornmeal bin began to get rather low. Father did not dare to venture into the woods in quest of game, for fear of the wolves, which every night would set up their hungry howling. Things were looking serious.

"One night we were all around the big fireplace. Father and Mother had a worried look on their faces. We children were a bit sober too—all but dusky little St. Pierre, or 'San Peter,' as my brothers had come to call the bright-eyed papoose. He was getting fun out of teasing the cat.

"Suddenly the little fellow jumped up and ran to the door. His keen ear had caught a sound of something. As he stood there listening intently, Father asked, 'What is it, San Peter?'

"'Somebody come; mebbe so Indians,' was the reply.

"We all were a bit startled. Father took his gun

from the fireplace, and took his stand by the door.
We all clustered round him, listening. Soon we
caught a sound of footsteps crunching through the
crusted snow. After a tense moment or two more,
there came a knock and Father demanded, 'Who is
it?'

" 'Bruere,' came the husky response.

"There was a glad exclamation from little San Peter, and a sigh of relief from us all as Father threw open the door. The flood of light from the fireplace showed two dusky, fur-clad forms, and behind them was a sled on which was a heavy load. It was old Bruere, indeed, and an Indian companion. They had battled their way through on their snowshoes to our home.

"After our welcome to them, they unloaded the sled. A big bundle of moccasins, and clothing made by the Indian mother, was first to be brought in; then came some warm furs and robes; and finally a large deer, with several big pieces of choice buffalo meat, was lifted inside! Oh, such a feast as we all had that night!

"Little San Peter and his sisters continued to live in our home and go to school with us until it closed that spring. Then our little French-Indian brother and sisters went back to their tepee home. We missed them greatly, especially bright-eyed San Peter, who was always keeping things lively for us by his happy mischief." *

* From *Living English* (Book Three) by Howard R. Driggs, published by The University Publishing Co.

LITTLE WOLFF'S WOODEN SHOES

Once upon a time—so long ago that everybody has forgotten the date—in a city in the northern part of Europe—whose name is so hard to pronounce that nobody remembers it—there lived a little boy seven years old whose name was Wolff.

He was an orphan and lived with an old aunt who was very cross and stingy. She kissed him but once a year, and that was on New Year's Day, and she breathed a sigh of regret every time she gave him a bowlful of soup.

But the poor little fellow had such a loving heart that he liked the old woman just the same in spite of the way she treated him.

Wolff's aunt would have liked to send him to school where the poor people sent their children. But she could not do it because everybody in the town knew that she owned her own house and had an old stocking full of gold.

But she quarreled with the school-master who taught the rich boys and made him take little Wolff as a pupil at reduced price. The school-master, vexed at having a pupil who came so poorly dressed

and paid so little, often punished little Wolff un-
justly. The school-master made him wear the dunce-
cap and even had the other boys make fun of him.

This made little Wolff as wretched as could be,
and he would hide himself in lonely corners to cry.
He always felt worse than ever at Christmas.

On one Christmas eve the school-master was to
take all his pupils to the midnight Mass, and then
take them home again.

It was a very cold night and the ground was covered with snow, so the boys came to the meeting
place warmly dressed. Their fur caps were pulled
down over their ears; they wore warm sweaters,
knitted gloves or mittens and sturdy boots with thick
soles. But poor little Wolff came shivering in his
everyday clothes and with coarse socks and a pair
of heavy wooden shoes on his feet.

The other pupils laughed at him because he looked
so poor and cold. But he was too busy blowing on
his hands to warm them, to pay any attention to the
taunts of the other boys. Then the boys, walking two
by two, with their teacher at the head of the line,
started for the church.

On the way to the church they boasted of the fine
suppers they should have when they got home.
The mayor's son had seen a big stuffed goose being

roasted. One of the other boys told of his Christmas
tree. Its branches were filled with oranges, candy
and jumping-jacks. Then the boys spoke, too, of
what the Christ Child would bring them, or what He
would leave in their shoes which they would set in
the fireplace before they went to bed. These little
fellows were active as a pack of mice, and their eyes
sparkled when they thought of the gifts they should
find when they awoke the next morning—pink bags
of burnt almonds, candy, sets of lead soldiers, painted
wooden animals, and jumping-jacks dressed in purple and tinsel.

Little Wolff knew very well that when he got home
his miserly aunt would send him supperless to bed.
He knew that he had been as good and had worked as
hard as possible all year. So he hoped that the Christ
Child would not forget him, and he, too, intended to
put his wooden shoes in the ashes of the fireplace
when he got home. At last the boys and their teacher
reached the church. It was warm and bright inside.

When the Mass was over, the people hurried home
to their suppers, and the pupils, walking two by two
after their teacher, left the church.

On a stone step of the church porch, a child was
sleeping. He was dressed in a white linen robe and
his feet were bare notwithstanding the cold. He was

not a beggar, for his robe was too clean and new, and near him on the ground were a hatchet, a pair of compasses, and other tools of a carpenter's apprentice. Under the light of the stars, his face bore an expression of divine sweetness, and his long locks of golden hair seemed to form a halo about his head. But it was pitiful to see the child's feet, blue in the cold of that December night.

The pupils, warmly dressed and well shod for the winter, passed the sleeping child without showing any pity. But little Wolff, the last of the pupils to come out of the church, stopped, deeply moved, before the beautiful sleeping child.

"Alas," the orphan said to himself, "it is a shame that this poor little boy has to go barefoot in such cold weather. But, what is still worse, he has no shoe to leave beside him while he is asleep, so that the Christ Child can put something in it to comfort him in his loneliness."

And so, little Wolff, carried away by his kindness of heart, took off the wooden shoe from his right foot and placed it near the sleeping child. Then, limping along and wetting his sock in the snow, he went home to his aunt.

"Look at the good-for-nothing!" cried the old woman, angry because one of his shoes was gone.

"What have you done with your shoe, little rascal?"

Trembling with terror, little Wolff tried to stammer out what had happened.

The miserly old woman burst into a frightful peal of laughter. "Oh, so the young gentleman gives his shoe to a beggar! That is very kind of him, indeed. And now since you did that, I am going to put the other wooden shoe before the fireplace, and the Christ Child will leave something in it to whip you with when you get up. Besides, you shall have nothing to eat to-morrow but bread and water. We shall see if next time you will give away your shoe to the first vagabond you meet!''

After having slapped the poor boy a couple of times, the aunt made him climb up to his wretched room in the attic. There the poor little fellow soon fell asleep, crying bitterly.

But the next morning, when the old woman went downstairs to the kitchen she saw—oh, wonderful sight!—the whole chimney-place full of beautiful toys, boxes of candy, and all sorts of fine things. And in front of all these things stood the wooden shoe which her nephew had given to the poor little boy and standing beside it, was the other shoe which she had placed there the night before, meaning to put a birch rod into it.

When little Wolff heard his aunt's cries of surprise, he came running downstairs. He too was delighted by the fine things in front of him. Suddenly they heard cries and shouts of laughter from out-of-doors. The old woman and the little boy went out to find out what it all meant, and they saw many people gathered around the public fountain. What could have happened? Oh, the most amusing and surprising thing. The rich children whose parents had intended to surprise them with wonderful gifts, had found only rods in their shoes.

Little Wolff and his aunt were amazed when they thought of all the beautiful things in their fireplace. But just then the priest came towards them with wonder in his face. In the church porch in the very place where the evening before a child dressed in white and with his bare feet exposed to the terrific cold, had rested his sleeping head, the priest had just seen a circle of gold graven into the old stone wall.

Then the people understood that the sleeping child near whom had lain the carpenter's tools, was Jesus Himself, and that He had returned to earth for an hour just as He was when He worked at the home of His parents, and they marveled at this miracle which the good God had been so kind as to perform to reward the faith and kindness of a little child.

TWO BOYS AVERT A WRECK

The following slightly adapted news story appeared not long since in one of the papers of the Middle West. Read it carefully, observing how clearly the reporter has pictured what happened.

Two Boys Avert Wreck

Red Sweater Waved When Giant Tree Found Felled Across Burlington Track

Two quick-witted boys and a red sweater averted what probably would have been a serious wreck on the Burlington near Camp Gifford early yesterday morning when they flagged fast passenger train No. 6, Chicago bound, in the nick of time to save it from crashing into a large tree lying across the rails.

The tree, a big cottonwood, had been felled across the track at a sharp curve and was obscured from view of the engineer, Charles Snyder of Lincoln, on the onrushing train which had left Omaha at seven.

James Caldwell and Clarence Swingholm, both thirteen, had left Camp Gifford and were tramping

194

about in the woods near the track when they discovered the giant tree. Persons searching for wild honey are believed to have chopped it down. Evidently it had not fallen in the direction planned, and the choppers, fearing the consequences, had fled.

To the north the lads could hear the rumble of No. 6, bearing down upon them with its load of unsuspecting passengers.

Failing in their efforts to move the tree, the pair dashed up the track, one of the boys jerking off his red sweater as he ran. Wildly they waved the improvised danger signal in the path of the train rushing toward the obstruction with unslackening speed.

The engineer saw the signal; his hand shot forward, and the "air" went on. With brakes shrieking, the heaving train came to a halt with the pilot of the huge locomotive opposite the scouts at the side of the track.

Dropping down from the cab, the engineer, followed by the fireman, crew, and badly shaken-up passengers, approached the two flushed lads.

"What's up, boys?" he demanded.

Two index fingers pointed down the track in the direction of the fallen tree.

The grimy hand of the engineer gripped those of the two small heroes. Passengers showered praise

upon the somewhat discomfited lads, several women expressing their appreciation by bestowing kisses on the two chubby faces.

A few minutes' work by the crew cleared the obstruction from the track, and the long train moved forward as passengers waved a farewell to the two boys.

Prompt action of the boys undoubtedly averted a serious wreck with possible loss of life, according to E. L. Underwood, special agent for the Burlington, who made a trip of inspection to the scene.*

A BOY'S SONG

Where the pools are bright and deep,
Where the gray trout lies asleep,
Up the river and o'er the lea,
That's the way for Billy and me.

Where the blackbird sings the latest,
Where the hawthorn blooms the sweetest,
Where the nestlings chirp and flee,
That's the way for Billy and me.

Where the mowers mow the cleanest,
Where the hay lies thick and greenest,
There to trace the homeward bee,
That's the way for Billy and me.

Where the hazel bank is steepest,
Where the shadow falls the deepest,
Where the clustering nuts fall free,
That's the way for Billy and me.

* From *Living English* (Third Book) by Howard R. Driggs, published by The University Publishing Co.

THE WIND AND THE MOON

Said the Wind to the Moon, "I will blow you out;
        You stare
        In the air
        Like a ghost in a chair,
Always looking what I am about—
I hate to be watched; I'll blow you out."

The Wind blew hard, and out went the Moon.
        So, deep
        On a heap
        Of clouds to sleep,
Down lay the Wind, and slumbered soon,
Muttering low, "I've done for that Moon."

He turned in his bed; she was there again!
        On high
        In the sky,
        With her one ghost eye,
The Moon shone white and alive and plain.
Said the Wind, "I will blow you out again."

The Wind blew hard, and the Moon grew dim.
>"With my sledge,
>And my wedge,
>I have knocked off her edge!
If only I blow right fierce and grim,
The creature will soon be dimmer than dim."

He blew and he blew, and she thinned to a thread.
>"One puff
>More's enough
>To blow her to snuff!
One good puff more where the last was bred,
And glimmer, glimmer, glum will go the thread."

He blew a great blast, and the thread was gone.
>In the air
>Nowhere
>Was a moonbeam bare;
Far off and harmless the shy stars shone—
Sure and certain the Moon was gone!

The Wind he took to his revels once more;
>On down,
>In town,
>Like a merry-mad clown,
He leaped and halloed with whistle and roar—
"What's that?" The glimmering thread once
   more!

He fled in a rage— he danced and blew;
>> But in vain
>> Was the pain
>> Of his bursting brain;
For still the broader the Moon-scrap grew,
The broader he swelled his big cheeks and blew.

Slowly she grew—till she filled the night,
>> And shone
>> On her throne
>> In the sky alone,
A matchless, wonderful silvery light,
Radiant and lovely, the queen of the night.

Said the Wind: "What a marvel of power am I!
>> With my breath,
>> Good faith!
>> I blew her to death—
First blew her away right out of the sky—
Then blew her in; what strength have I!"

But the Moon she knew nothing about the affair;
>> For high
>> In the sky,
>> With her one white eye,
Motionless, miles above the air,
She had never heard the great Wind blare.

THE CLOCKS OF RONDAINE

I

Centuries ago, there stood on the banks of a river a little town called Rondaine. The river was a long and winding stream which ran through different countries, and was sometimes narrow and swift, and sometimes broad and placid; sometimes hurrying through mountain passes, and again meandering quietly through fertile plains; in some places of a blue color and almost transparent, and in others of a dark and somber hue; and so it changed until it threw itself into a warm far-spreading sea.

But it was quite otherwise with the little town. As far back as anybody could remember, it had always been the same that it was at the time of our story; and the people who lived there could see no reason to suppose that it would ever be different from what it was then. It was a pleasant little town, its citizens were very happy; and why there should be any change in it, the most astute old man in all Rondaine could not have told you.

If Rondaine had been famed for anything at all, it would have been for the number of its clocks. It had many churches, some little ones in dark side streets, and some larger ones in wider avenues, besides here and there a very good-sized church fronting on a park or open square; and in the steeple of each of these churches there was a clock.

There were town buildings, very old ones, which

stood upon the great central square. Each of these
had a tower, and in each tower was a clock.

Then there were clocks at street corners, and two
clocks in the market place, and clocks over shop
doors, a clock at each end of the bridge, and several
large clocks a little way out of town. Many of these
clocks were fashioned in some quaint and curious
way. In one of the largest a stone man came out
and struck the hours with a stone hammer, while a
stone woman struck the half-hours with a stone
broom; and in another an iron donkey kicked the
hours on a bell behind him.

It would be impossible to tell all the odd ways in
which the clocks of Rondaine struck; but in one re-
spect they were alike; they all did strike. The good
people of the town would not have tolerated a clock
which did not strike.

It was very interesting to lie awake in the night
and hear the clocks of Rondaine strike. First would
come a faint striking from one of the churches in the
by-streets, a modest sound, as if the clock was not
sure whether it was too early or not; then from another quarter would be heard a more confident clock
striking the hour clearly and distinctly.

When they were quite ready, but not a moment
before, the seven bells of a large church on the square

would chime the hour; after which, at a respectful interval of time, the other church clocks of the town would strike. After the lapse of three or four minutes, the sound of all these bells seemed to wake up the stone man in the tower of the town building and he struck the hour with his hammer. When this had been done, the other town clocks felt at liberty to strike, and they did so. And when every sound had died away, so that he would be certain to be heard if there was any one awake to hear, it would be very likely that the iron donkey would kick out the hour on his bell. But there were times when he kicked before any of the clocks began to strike.

One by one the clocks on the street corners struck, the uptown ones first, and afterward those near the river. These were followed by the two clocks on the bridge, the one at the country end waiting until it was quite sure that the one at the town end had finished. Somewhat later would be heard the clock of Vougereau, an old country-house in the suburbs. This clock, a very large one, was on the top of a great square stone tower, and from its age it had acquired a habit of deliberation; and when it began to strike, people were very apt to think that it was one o'clock, until after an interval another stroke would tell them that it was later or earlier than that, and if they really wanted to know what hour the old clock was striking, they must give themselves time enough to listen until they were entirely certain that it had finished.

The very last clock to strike in Rondaine was one belonging to a little old lady with white hair, who lived in a little white house in one of the prettiest and cleanest streets in the town. Her clock was in a little white tower at the corner of her house and was the only strictly private clock which was in the habit of making itself publicly heard. Long after every other clock had struck, and when there was every reason to believe that for some time nothing but half-hours would be heard in Rondaine, the old lady's clock would strike quickly and with a tone that said, ''I know I am right, and I wish other people to know it.''

In a small house which stood at the corner of two streets in the town there lived a young girl named Arla. For a year or more this young girl had been in the habit of waking up very early in the morning, sometimes long before daylight, and it had become a habit with her to lie and listen to the clocks. Her room was at the top of the house, and one of its windows opened to the west and another to the south, so that sounds entered from different quarters. Arla

liked to leave these windows open so that the sounds
of the clocks might come in.

Arla knew every clock by its tone, and she always
made it a point to lie awake until she was positively
sure that the last stroke of the clock at Vougereau
had sounded. But it often happened that sleep over-
came her before she heard the clock of the little old
lady with the white hair. It was so very long to wait
for that!

It was not because she wanted to know the hour
that Arla used to lie and listen to the clocks. She
could tell this from her own little clock in her room.
This little clock, which had been given to her when
she was a small girl, not only struck the hours and
half-hours and quarter-hours, but there was attached
to it a very pretty contrivance, which also told the
time. On the front of the clock, just below the dial
was a sprig of a rosebush beautifully made of metal,
and on this, just after the hour had sounded, there
was a large green bud; at a quarter past the hour
this bud opened a little, so that the red petals could
be seen; fifteen minutes later it was a half-blown rose,
and at a quarter of an hour more it was nearly full
blown; just before the hour the rose opened to its
fullest extent, and so remained until the clock had
finished striking, when it immediately shut up into a

great green bud. This clock was a great delight to Arla, for not only was it a very pleasant thing to watch the unfolding of the rose, but it was a continual satisfaction to her to think that her little clock always told her exactly what time it was, no matter what the other clocks of Rondaine might say.

II

Arla's father and mother were thrifty, industrious people, who were very fond of their daughter, and wished her to grow up a thoughtful, useful woman. In the very early morning, listening to the clocks of Rondaine or waiting for them, Arla did a great deal of thinking; and so it happened, on the morning of the day before Christmas, when the stars were bright and the air frosty, and every outside sound very clear and distinct, that Arla began to think of something which had never entered her mind before.

"How in the world," she said to herself, "do the people of Rondaine know when it is really Christmas? Christmas begins as soon as it is twelve o'clock on Christmas Eve; but as some of the people depend for the time upon one clock and some upon others, a great many of them cannot truly know when

Christmas has come, when in reality it is yet the day before. And not one of them strikes at the right time! As for that iron donkey, I believe he kicks whenever he feels like it. And yet there are people who go by him! I know this, for they have told me so. But the little old lady with white hair is worse off than anybody else. Christmas must always come ever so long before she knows it.''

With these thoughts on her mind, Arla could not go to sleep again. She heard all the clocks strike, and lay awake until her own little clock told her that she ought to get up. During this time she had made up her mind what she would do. There was yet one day before Christmas; and if the people of the town could be made to see in what a deplorable condition they were on account of the difference in their clocks, they might have time to set the matter right so that all the clocks should strike the correct hour, and everybody should know exactly when Christmas Day began. She was sure the citizens had never even given the matter proper thought; and it was quite natural that such should be the case, for it was not every one who was in the habit of lying awake in the very early morning; and in the daytime, with all the out-door noises, one could not hear all the clocks strike in Rondaine. Arla, therefore, thought that a great deal depended upon her, who knew exactly how this matter stood.

When she went down to breakfast she asked permission of her mother to take a day's holiday. As she was a good girl, and never neglected either her lessons or her tasks, her mother was quite willing to give her the day before Christmas in which she could do as she pleased.

The day was cool, but the sun shone brightly and the air was pleasant. In the country around about Rondaine Christmas-time was not a very cold season. Arla put on a warm jacket and a pretty blue hood, and started out gayly to attend to the business in hand.

Everybody in Rondaine knew her father and mother, and a great many of them knew her, so there was no reason why she should be afraid to go where she chose. In one hand she carried a small covered basket, in which she had placed her rose-clock. The works of this little clock were regulated by a balance-wheel, like those of a watch, and therefore it could be carried about without stopping it.

The first place she visited was the church at which she and her parents always attended service. It was a small building in a little square at the bottom of a hill, and, to reach it, one had to go down a long flight of stone steps. When she entered the dimly lighted church, Arla soon saw the sacristan, a pleasant faced little old man whom she knew very well.

"Good morning, sir," she said. "Do you take care of the church clock?"

The sacristan was sweeping the stone pavements of the church, just inside the door. He stopped and leaned upon his broom. "Yes, my little friend," he said, "I take care of everything here except the souls of the people."

"Well, then," said Arla, "I think you ought to know that your clock is eleven minutes fast. I came here to tell you that, so that you might change it, and make it strike properly."

The sacristan's eyes began to twinkle. He was a man of merry mood. "That is very good of you, little Arla; very good indeed. And, now that we are about it, isn't there something else you would like to change? What do you say to having these stone pillars put to one side, so that they may be out of the way of the people when they come in? Or those great beams in the roof—they might be turned over, and perhaps we might find that the upper side would look fresher than this lower part, which is somewhat time-stained, as you see? Or, for the matter of that, what do you say to having our clock tower taken down and set out there in the square before the church door? The short-sighted people could see the time much better, don't you think? Now, tell me, shall we do all these things together, wise little friend?"

A tear or two came into Arla's eyes, but she made no answer.

"Good morning, sir," she said, and went away.

"I suppose," she said to herself as she ran up the stone steps, "that he thought it would be too much trouble to climb to the top of the tower to set the clock right. But that was no reason why he should make fun of me. I don't like him as much as I used to."

The next church to which Arla went was a large one, and it was some time before she could find the sacristan. At last she saw him in a side chapel at the upper end of the church, engaged in dusting some old books. He was a large man, with a red face, and he turned around quickly, with a stern expression, as she entered.

"Please, sir," said Arla, "I came to tell you that your church clock is wrong. It strikes from four to six minutes before it ought to; sometimes the one and sometimes the other. It should be changed so that it will be sure to strike at the right time."

The face of the sacristan grew redder and twitched visibly at her remark.

"Do you know what I wish?" he shouted in reply.

"No, sir," answered Arla.

"I wish," he said, "that you were a boy, so that I might take you by the collar and soundly cuff your ears, for coming here to insult an officer of the church in the midst of his duties! But, as you are a girl, I can only tell you to go away from here as rapidly and as quietly as you can, or I shall have to put you in the hands of the church authorities!"

Arla was truly frightened, and although she did not run—for she knew that would not be proper in a church—she walked as fast as she could into the outer air.

"What a bad man," she then said to herself, "to be employed in a church! It surely is not known what sort of person he is, or he would not be allowed to stay there a day!"

Arla thought she would not go to any more churches at present, for she did not know what sort of sacristans she might find in them.

"When the other clocks in the town all strike properly," she thought, "it is most likely they will see for themselves that their clocks are wrong, and they will have them changed."

III

She now made her way to the great square of the town, and entered the building at the top of which stood the stone man with his hammer. She found the door-keeper in a little room by the side of the entrance. She knew where to go, for she had been there with her mother to ask permission to go up and see the stone man strike the hour with his hammer, and the stone woman strike the half-hour with her broom.

The door-keeper was a grave, middle-aged man with spectacles; and, remembering what had just happened, Arla thought she should be careful how she spoke to him.

"If you please, sir," she said, with a curtsy, "I should like to say something to you. And I hope you will not be offended when I tell you that your clock is not quite right. Your stone man and your stone woman are both too slow; they sometimes strike as much as seven minutes after they ought to strike."

The grave, middle-aged man looked steadily at her through his spectacles.

"I thought," continued Arla, "that if this should be made known to you, you would have the works of the stone man and the stone woman altered so that they might strike at the right time. They can be heard so far, you know, that it is very necessary they should not make mistakes."

"Child," said the man, with his spectacles still steadily fixed on her, "for one hundred and fifty-seven years the thunder and lightning in time of storm have roared and flashed around it, and the sun in time of fair weather has shone upon it. In that century and a half and seven years men and women have lived and died, and their children and their grandchildren and their great-grandchildren, and even the children of these, have lived and died after them. Kings and queens have passed away, one after another; and all things living have grown old and died, one generation after another, many times. And yet, through all these years, that stone man and that stone woman have stood there, and in storm and in fair weather, by daylight or in the darkness of night, they have struck the hours and the half hours. Of all things that one hundred and fifty-seven years ago were able to lift an arm to strike, they alone are left. And now you, a child of thirteen, or perhaps fourteen years, come to me and ask me to change that which has not been changed for a century and a half and seven years!''

Arla could answer nothing with those spectacles fixed upon her. They seemed to glare more and more as she looked at them. ''Good morning, sir,'' she said, dropping a curtsy as she moved backward towards the door. Reaching it, she turned and hurried into the street.

''If those stone people,'' she thought, ''have not been altered in all these years, it is likely they would now be striking two or three hours out of the way! But I don't know. If they kept on going slow for more than a century, they must have come around to the right hour sometimes. But they will have to strike ever and ever so much longer before they come around there again!''

Arla now walked on until she came to a street corner where a cobbler had a little shop. In the angle of the wall of the house, at the height of the second story, was a clock. This cobbler did not like the confined air and poor light of his shop and, whenever the weather allowed, he always worked outside on the sidewalk.

To-day, although it was winter, the sun shone brightly on this side of the street, and he had put his bench outside, close to the door, and was sitting there,

hard at work. When Arla stopped before him, he looked up and said cheerfully:

"Good-morning, Mistress Arla. Do you want them half-soled, or heeled, or a patch put on the toes?"

"My shoes do not need mending," said Arla. "I came to ask you if you could tell me who has charge of the clock at this corner?"

"I can easily do that," he said, "for I am the man. I am paid by the year for winding it up and keeping it in order, as much as I should get for putting the soles, heels, tops, linings and buckles on a pair of shoes."

"Which means making them out and out," said Arla.

"You are right," said he, "and the pay is not great; but if it were larger, more people might want it and I might lose it; and if it were less, how could I afford to do it all? So I am satisfied."

"But you ought not to be entirely satisfied," said Arla, "for the clock does not keep good time. I know when it is striking, for it has a very jangling sound and it is the most irregular clock in Rondaine. Sometimes it strikes as much as twenty-five minutes after the hour, and very often it does not strike at all."

The cobbler looked up at her with a smile. "I am sorry, but the fashioning of the clocks is not my trade, and I could not mend its sound with awl, hammer or waxed end. But it seems to me, my good maiden, that you never mended a pair of shoes."

"No, indeed!" said Arla: "I should do that even worse than you would make clocks."

"Never having mended shoes, then," said the cobbler, "you do not know what a grievous thing it is to have twelve o'clock or six o'clock or any other hour,

in fact, come before you are ready for it. Now, I
don't mind telling you, because I know you are too
good to spoil the trade of a hard-working cobbler—
and shoe-maker, too, whenever he gets the chance
to be one—that when I have promised a customer
that he shall have his shoes or his boots at a certain
time of day, and that time is drawing near, and the
end of the job is still somewhat distant, then do I
skip up the stairway and set back the hands of the
clock according to the work that has to be done. And
when my customer comes I look up to the clock face
and I say to him, 'Glad to see you!' and then he will
look up at the clock and will say, 'Yes, I am a little
too soon'; and then, as likely as not, he will sit down
on the doorstep here by me and talk entertainingly;
and it may happen that he will sit there without
grumbling for many minutes after the clock has
pointed out the hour at which the shoes were promised.

"Sometimes when I have been much belated in
beginning a job, I stop the clock altogether, for you
can well see for yourself, that it would not do to have
it strike eleven when it is truly twelve. And so, if
my man be willing to sit down, and our talk be very
entertaining, the clock being above him where he
cannot see it without stepping outward from the

house, he may not notice that it is stopped. This once served me very well, for an old gentleman, over-testy and over-punctual, once came to me for his shoes and, looking up at the clock, which I had pre-pared for him, exclaimed, 'Bless me! I am much too early!' And he sat down by me for three-quarters of an hour, in which time I persuaded him that his shoes were far too much worn to be worth mending any more, and that he should have a new pair, which afterward I made.''

"I do not believe it is right for you to do that," said Arla; "but even if you think so, there is no reason why your clock should go wrong at night, when so many people can hear it because of the still-ness."

"Ah, me!" said the cobbler, "I do not object to the clock being as right as you please in the night; but when my day's work is done, I am in such a hurry to go home to my supper that I often forget to put the clock right, or to set it going if it is stopped. But so many things stop at night—such as the day itself —and so many things even go wrong—such as the ways of evil-minded people—that I think you truly ought to pardon my poor clock."

"Then you will not consent," said Arla, "to make it go right?"

"I will do that with all cheerfulness," answered the cobbler, pulling out a pair of wax-ends with a great jerk, "as soon as I can make myself go right. The most important thing should always be done first; and, surely, I am more important than a clock!" And he smiled with great good humor.

Arla knew that it would be no use to stand there any longer and talk with the cobbler. Turning to go, she said:

"When I bring you shoes to mend, you shall finish them by my clock, and not by yours."

"That will I, my good little Arla," said the cobbler heartily. "They shall be finished by any clock in town, and five minutes before the hour, or no payment."

Arla now walked on until she came to the bridge over the river. It was a long covered bridge, and by the entrance sat the bridge-keeper.

"Do you know, sir," said she, "that the clock at this end of the bridge does not keep the same time as the one at the other? They are not so very different, but I have noticed that this one is always done striking at least two minutes before the other begins."

The bridge-keeper looked at her with one eye, which was all he had.

"You are as wrong as anybody can be," said he. "I do not say anything about the striking, because my ears are not now good enough to hear the clock at the other end when I am near this one; but I know they both keep the same time. I have often looked at this clock and have then walked to the other end of the bridge, and have found that the clock there was exactly like it."

Arla looked at the poor little man, whose legs were warmly swaddled on account of his rheumatism, and said:

"But it must take you a good while to walk to the other end of the bridge."

"Out upon you!" cried the bridge-keeper. "I am not so old as that yet! I can walk there in no time!"

Arla now crossed the bridge and went a short distance along a country road until she came to the great stone house known as Vougereau. This be-longed to a rich family who seldom went there, and the place was in charge of an elderly man who was the brother of Arla's mother. When his niece was shown into a room on the ground floor, which served for his parlor and his office, he was very glad to see her; and while Arla was having something to eat and drink after her walk, the two had a pleasant chat.

"I came this time, Uncle Anton," said she, "not only to see you, but to tell you that the great clock in your tower does not keep good time."

Uncle Anton looked at her a little surprised.

"How do you know that, my dear?" he said.

Then Arla told him how she had lain awake in the early morning, and had heard the striking of the different clocks. "If you wish to make it right," said she, "I can give you the proper time, for I have brought my own little clock with me."

She was about to take her rose-clock out of her basket, when her uncle motioned to her not to do so.

"Let me tell you something," said he. "The altering of the time of day, which you speak of so lightly, is a very serious matter, which should be considered with all gravity. If you set back a clock, even as little as ten minutes, you add that much to the time that has passed. The hour which has just gone by has been made seventy minutes long. Now, no human being has the right to add anything to the past, nor to make hours longer than they were originally made. And, on the other hand, if you set a clock forward even so little as ten minutes, you take away that much from the future, and you make the coming hour only fifty minutes long. Now, no human being has a right to take anything away from the future, or to make the hours shorter than they were intended to be. I desire, my dear niece, that you will earnestly think over what I have said, and I am sure that you will then see for yourself how unwise it would be to trifle with the length of the hours which make up our day. And now, Arla, let us talk over other things.''

And so they talked of other things until Arla thought it was time to go. She saw there was something wrong in her uncle's reasoning, although she could not tell exactly what it was and, thinking about it, she slowly returned to the town. As she approached the house of the little old lady with white hair, she concluded to stop and speak to her about her clock. ''She will surely be willing to alter that,'' said Arla, ''for it is so very much out of the way.''

The old lady knew who Arla was, and received her very kindly; but when she heard why the young girl had come to her, she flew into a passion.

''Never since I was born,'' she said, ''have I been spoken to like this! My great-grandfather lived in this house before me; that clock was good enough for him! My father and mother lived in this house before me; that clock was good enough for them! I was born in this house, have always lived in it, and expect to die in it; that clock is good enough for me! I heard its strokes when I was but a little child, I hope to hear them at my last hour; and sooner than raise my hand against the clock of my ancestors, and the clock of my whole life, I would cut off that hand!"

Some tears came into Arla's eyes; she was a little frightened. "I hope you will pardon me, good madam," she said, "for, truly, I did not wish to offend you. Nor did I think that your clock was not a good one. I only meant that you should make it better; it is nearly an hour out of the way."

The sight of Arla's tears cooled the anger of the little old lady with white hair. "Child," she said, "you do not know what you are talking about, and I forgive you. But remember this: never ask persons as old as I am to alter the principles which have always made clear to them what they should do, or the clocks which have always told them when they should do it."

And, kissing Arla, she bade her good-by.

"Principles may last a great while without altering," thought Arla, as she went away, "but I am sure it is very different with clocks."

The poor girl now felt a good deal discouraged.

"The people don't seem to care whether their clocks are right or not," she said to herself, "and if they don't care, I am sure it is of no use for me to tell them about it. If even one clock could be made

to go properly, it might help to make the people of
Rondaine care to know exactly what time it is. Now,
there is that iron donkey. If he would kick at the
right hour it would be an excellent thing, for he kicks
so hard that he is heard all over the town.''

Determined to make this one more effort, Arla
walked quickly to the town building, at the top of
which was the clock with the iron donkey. This
building was a sort of museum; it had a great many
curious things in it, and it was in charge of a very
ingenious man, who was learned and skillful in
various ways.

When Arla had informed the superintendent of
the museum why she had come to him, he did not
laugh at her nor did he get angry. He was accus-
tomed to giving earnest consideration to matters of
this sort, and he listened to all that Arla had
to say.

''You must know,'' he said, ''that our iron donkey
is a very complicated piece of mechanism. Not only
must he kick out the hours, but five minutes before
doing so he must turn his head around and look at
the bell behind him; and then, when he has done
kicking, he must put his head back into its former
position. All this action requires a great many wheels
and cogs and springs and levers and these cannot

be made to move with absolute regularity. When it is cold, some of his works contract; and when it is warm they expand; and there are other reasons why he is very likely to lose or gain time. At noon, on every bright day, I set him right, being able to get the correct time from a sun-dial which stands in the court-yard. But his works—which I am sorry to say are not well made—are sure to get a great deal out of the way before I set him again.''

"Then, if there are several cloudy or rainy days together, he goes very wrong indeed," said Arla.

"Yes, he truly does," replied the superintendent, "and I am sorry for it. But there is no way to help it except for me to make him all over again at my own expense, and that is something I cannot afford to do. The clock belongs to the town, and I am sure the citizens will not be willing to spend the money necessary for a new donkey-clock; for, so far as I know, every person but yourself is perfectly satisfied with this one."

"I suppose so," said Arla, with a sigh: "but it really is a great pity that every striking-clock in Rondaine should be wrong!"

"But how do you know that they are all wrong?" asked the superintendent.

"Oh, that is easy enough," said Arla. "When I lie awake in the early morning, when all else is very still, I listen to their striking, and then I look at my own rose-clock to see what time it really is."

"Your rose-clock?" said the superintendent.

"This is it," said Arla opening her basket and taking out her little clock.

The superintendent took into his hands and looked at it attentively, both outside and inside. And then, still holding it, he stepped out into the court-yard.

When in a few moments he returned, he said:
"I have compared your clock with my sun-dial and
found that it is ten minutes slow. I also see that,
like the donkey-clock its works are not adjusted in
such a way as to be unaffected by heat and cold."

"My clock—ten—minutes—slow!" exclaimed Arla
with wide-open eyes.

"Yes," said the superintendent, "that is the case
to-day, and on some days, it is probably a great deal
too fast. Such a clock as this—which is a very ingenious and beautiful one—ought frequently to be
compared with a sun-dial or other correct time-
keeper, and set to the proper hour. I see it requires
a peculiar key with which to set it. Have you brought
this with you?"

"No, sir," said Arla; "I did not suppose it would
be needed."

"Well, then," said the superintendent, "you can
set it forward ten minutes when you reach home;
and if to-morrow morning you compare the other
clocks with it, I think you will find that not all of
them are wrong."

Arla sat quiet for a moment and then she said: "I
think I shall not care to compare the clocks of Rondaine with my little rose-clock. If the people are
satisfied with their own clocks, whether they are fast

or slow, and do not care to know exactly when
Christmas Day begins, I can do nobody any good
by listening to the different strikings and then
looking at my own little clock, with a night-lamp
by it."

"Especially," said the superintendent, with a
smile, "when you are not sure that your rose-clock is
right. But if you bring here your little clock and
your key on any day when the sun is shining, I will
set it to the time shadowed on the sun-dial, or show
you how to do it yourself."

"Thank you very much," said Arla, and she took
her leave.

As she walked home, she lifted the lid of her basket
and looked at her little rose-clock. "To think of it!"
she said. "That you should be sometimes too fast
and sometimes too slow! And, worse than that, to
think that some of the other clocks have been right
and you have been wrong! But I do not feel like
altering you to-day. If you go fast sometimes, and
slow sometimes, you must be right sometimes, and
one of these days, when I take you to be compared
with the sun-dial, perhaps you will not have to be
altered so much."

Arla went to bed that night quite tired with her
long walks, and when she awoke it was broad

daylight. "I do not know," she said to herself, "exactly when Christmas began, but I am very sure that the happy day is here."

"Do you lie awake in the morning as much as you used to?" asked Arla's mother, a few weeks after the Christmas holidays.

"No, Mother dear," said Arla; "I now sleep with one of my windows shut, and I am no longer awakened by that chilly feeling which used to come to me in the early morning, when I would draw the bedcovers close about me and think how wrong were the clocks of Rondaine."

And the little rose-clock never went to be compared with the sun-dial. "Perhaps you are right now," Arla would say to her clock each day when the sun shone, "and I will not take you until some time when I feel very sure that you are wrong."

THE VISION OF SIR LAUNFAL

I

Opportunity for service lies at our door, and we **need** not seek far for great things to do.

This story begins in the summer time when every-body and everything was bright and happy. The flowers were blooming, the birds were singing, and every leaf and blade of grass made a home for some little creature.

Amidst all the joy of summer time a great castle stretched its towers toward the sky, gray and cold. It was not at all like the beautiful summer. It looked like winter. It was a proud old castle and its gates were opened only to admit rich lords and ladies. The poor were always turned away.

A young knight named Sir Launfal lived in this castle. He was strong and brave and very proud of his old home. He was a good young man but he had not yet learned to be kind to the poor. He decided to travel the world over seeking for something **to** do that would please God. He had his beautiful armor brought out and everything made ready for an early start one summer morning. Then he threw himself down on his bed for a few hours' sleep.

Around the castle was a ditch, which was crossed by a drawbridge. This was let down by chains, but when it was up no man could leave the castle. As Sir Launfal rode across this bridge the next morning, the sun shone upon his armor turning it to gold, and he felt so strong and happy that it was a joy just to be alive. The birds were singing in the tall trees of the forest around his castle; the cattle were peacefully grazing in the meadows, the flowers were blooming. The knight looked up at the blue sky, and said: "I want to do some great thing for my Lord." He was thinking of some great victory in battle over many enemies, and hardly looked down at the road under his feet.

As he came out from the castle he came upon a leper, a poor man, ragged and dirty, and sick with a dreadful disease. He was lying on the side of the road and was very pitiful in his poverty. Now, it was the custom for those who were lepers or were very poor to lie at the gates of the castle and beg for food or money, or for anything that would be given them. So this leper cried out to the young man:

"Sir Knight, help me in the name of the Master!"

Sir Launfal looked down at the poor beggar, and the sunshine went out of his heart. Instead of helping the man, he scornfully tossed him a piece of gold and turned away. The leper did not pick up the gold. He would rather have had a kind word even from the poor, than unwilling gold from the rich.

Sir Launfal rode on looking for a great adventure, while the gold lay untouched on the ground and the leper turned sadly away. To-morrow we shall see how Sir Launfal learned to serve the Lord in the right way.

II

Performing the simple service at our hands brings more real joy than. mighty conquests abroad.

Years passed by while Sir Launfal wandered far and wide, but never found the great things he sought to do. He fought many battles and he endured great hardships in the deserts, but somehow it did not bring him peace of mind that he sought. Try as he might to do som' great deed, he did not please God and he was down ast and discouraged. He had spent all his money and had only his horse, his armor, and a crust of bread.

At last he turned homeward, but found that the people, thinking that he was dead, had taken his home from him. When he tried to enter his castle they turned him away.

It was winter time. The wind blew loud and cold. Poor Sir Launfal had no home. He drew his cloak around him and looked through the windows into his castle. It was Christmas, all the rooms were trimmed with holly. He saw the great fire burning but could not get warm. He tried to forget the bitter cold by remembering how the hot sun shone down on the desert. As he was thinking, he heard a voice say:

"For Jesus' sake, help me!" He saw near him the
same poor leper who had begged for help when he
rode away from his castle that summer morning. He
also remembered how he had treated him and felt
very sorry that he had not been more kind and loving.

"You poor beggar," said he. "I am hardly more than a beggar myself now, and I have not much to give, but I will divide what I have."

So he divided his crust of bread, which was all he had, then broke the ice on the brook and gave the leper a drink. It seemed to the leper that he had never tasted anything so good. As he ate the bread and drank the water it seemed to Sir Launfal that the peace and joy he had been years trying to find had at last come into his heart.

Suddenly a beautiful light shone upon Sir Launfal and looking up, he saw—not a poor leper—but Jesus Christ Himself! Gently He spoke:

"Be not afraid, Sir Launfal; over all the world you have searched in vain for one thing to do for Me, while here at your own gate, are the sick and poor whom you could love and help."

Then Sir Launfal awoke, and found that all this had been a dream, and that he had never ridden forth from the castle at all. But he felt sure that the dream had been sent to teach him not to be proud and selfish. He called to his servants and said:

"Hang up my armor, for I am not going to travel. Instead, I shall hereafter be kind to all the poor who come to my gates." Then he found the great service he longed to do for the Master.

THE 100% GOOD TURN

Tony still had a knot tied in his blue neckerchief and that meant this tenderfoot had not yet done his daily "good turn." It was after nine p. m. The weekly Troop Meeting had broken up ten minutes ago in a riot of shouts and scramblings, when the Scoutmaster had threatened: "The last one out of this hall goes under the mill."

Tony had been second last out. It had been a close call, for his Troop fellows always willingly supplied the paddle power for the "mill."

Now Tony was passing in front of St. Anthony's Church. His hand went up and his hat came off reverently to his Friend in the Tabernacle. Just where the light from the street lamp fell strongest, Tony saw something white. He reached down and picked up an open envelope. The address had been torn off and Tony was about to throw the envelope away when he noticed there was a letter within.

Tony was as curious as his white kitten "Snowball. So he stood under the street light and

unfolded the letter. It was poorly printed on cheap paper. It began:

"Dear Friend,

"No one knows better than I, the many calls made on your charity; yet I trust you will be patient with me for making the following appeal for my little church and congregation here in Gastonia, N. C."

The letter went on to tell how the priest had many demands on his funds. The people were very poor.

There were many children, but no parochial school for them. Any sum to build it would be welcome. The letter ended:

> "Your love for souls and zeal for the spreading of our Holy Faith will not, I trust, permit you to forget the humble appeal of a poor priest. All I can do for you will be to pray for you and to ask the prayers of my little flock, and this I shall do."

The letter was signed "Rev. Anthony O'Brien, O.S.B., St. Anthony's Church, Gastonia, N. C."

There was something in the strange letter that touched Tony. He had secret hopes of some day being a "Father Anthony" himself. He wished just now that he was a millionaire, like Mr. Dignan, the banker, who lived in the big brown stone house down the street from Tony's home. Then he could sit down, take out his check book, and write out a check for $1000. "But that's a bedtime fairy tale for me," thought Tony. He was not poor, but he did not have a check book. Standing there, Tony's hand went up to his throat and happened to touch the knot in his neckerchief. Tony whistled, for that knot was tied there to remind Tony of something. It meant he had not yet done his daily "good turn."

Now Tony was on his way home to bed. It would never do to omit that "good turn." Faithfully he had done one daily since he had been admitted into the parish Troop.

Tony looked wildly about him. There was no blind man in need of assistance nearby. There was no crying lost child. There was no old lady standing on the corner, waiting to be helped across the crowded street. If there had been a lady the age of Tony's grandmother, she could have crossed that shadowed avenue without the faintest danger from traffic at that hour of the night. The only automobile Tony could see had its parking lights burning in front of Hansen's Drug Store.

Tony remembered he intended to stop in at the drug store and get a quarter's worth of chocolates. In his breeches' pocket was the last dollar of the five Aunt Polly had given him on his recent birthday.

There came to Tony a sudden thought. It was a disagreeable thought at first. It meant no candy to-night and the rest of the week. But it certainly would be a real "good turn."

In doubt, Tony looked back towards St. Anthony's Church. From where he stood, he could see in through the window the faithful red lamp that burnt before the Tabernacle.

"That Father O'Brien could use a dollar," thought Tony, "Doesn't this letter say the smallest sum will be gratefully received?"

Yet a chocolate drop would taste good. Tony licked his lips hungrily and thought of breakfast, which was long hours away. The words of The Law flashed up in his mind,—"He must do at least one Good Turn to somebody every day."

"I keep my promise," the scout murmured.

With this he straightened up. His right hand came smartly up to the brim of his hat, thumb covering the nail of the little finger, and he saluted in the general direction of that red sanctuary light.

"All right, Good Jesus. That dollar goes to North Carolina and this altar boy of Yours writes the letter to-night before he gets into bed."

Somehow, Tony felt happier as he hurried home. It was not so hard to pass the brilliantly lighted drug store on the next corner. Tony turned into his home and went up to his room. He threw his scout hat and neckerchief on the bed and got out his box of writing paper.

When the letter was written to the strange priest in North Carolina, Tony put his last dollar bill in the envelope. Then he went over, untied the knot in his blue neckerchief, said his night prayers, and got

into bed. Having a very good conscience, he was sound asleep three minutes later.

In the morning, on the way to school, Tony intended to stop at the Post Office and get a money order for one dollar. But Tony's mother had buckwheat cakes and country sausage for breakfast and, somehow, Tony was eight minutes late starting for school. He would have to wait till after school to get that money order, he thought, as he ran rapidly down the block.

Just then a horn honked and a desert gray roadster turned into the curb beside him.

"Hello, Tony," called out Mr. Dignan from the car, "you seem to be in a hurry. I had to step on it to catch up with you. May I do my 'good turn' early and give you a lift to school?"

"Can you! It's done, sir," cried Tony, dropping gratefully into the vacant seat alongside Mr. Dignan, who was an active member, of the Boy Scout Troop Committee.

In no time Tony was telling the banker that he had planned to go to the Post Office before school, but buckwheat cakes and country sausages had prevented.

When Mr. Dignan learned Tony wanted a money order for one dollar, he suggested another plan.

"Give me that dollar bill and when I get to the bank I'll make out my check for the amount and enclose it in your letter. How is that?"

Tony smiled his best scout smile. "It suits me, Mr. Dignan, and besides you save me five cents for the money order."

So Tony passed the addressed envelope and the dollar bill over to his friend the banker. At his school corner, he thanked Mr. Dignan for the ride. Then he had to run, for the last bell was ringing.

Mr. Dignan forgot all about Tony's letter till late that afternoon, when he pulled it out of his pocket. At first, the banker did not recognize it. He opened the envelope and read this letter:

"Dear Father Anthony O'Brien:

"I found your letter on the street this evening and here is some money I had. I want you to use it for your poor children.

"Your scout friend,

"Tony

"P. S.

"Don't forget the prayers you promised to say for any one who sent you something for your poor children. My batting eye needs to improve *very much.*"

Then Mr. Dignan saw the folded dollar bill within the envelope and he remembered his promise to Tony.

The banker reached for his check book. He dated the check. Then he wrote in the name,

"Rev. Anthony O'Brien, O.S.B."

Here Mr. Dignan stopped and began drumming on his polished desk.

He knew a dollar was a large sum to Tony. It must have cost the lad something to give it away.

Mr. Dignan looked at another letter lying before him. He knew it was waiting till he enclosed a check for one hundred dollars for that specially matched set of golf sticks he had wanted.

Again Mr. Dignan read Tony's letter, this time very carefully.

"That little Tenderfoot is doing a 'good turn' that is costing him something! He called me a good scout when I gave him a lift to school this morning. Well, a good scout does a 'good turn' daily." He reached over and tore up the letter to the Universal Sporting Goods Company. He murmured as he dropped the scraps of paper into the waste basket, "I guess I can get along with my present sticks."

Then Mr. Dignan took Tony's dollar bill and, folding it neatly, put it in his wallet. Picking up his fountain pen he filled in the amount on Tony's check.

It was for just one hundred times the sum that Tony had given!

On his way home the banker stopped at a green letter box and posted Tony's letter.

Passing the school yard he noticed a ball game was over and he slowed down his roadster as he saw the boy he had been thinking about.

"Hop in, Tony, and I'll give you a lift to your home."

"Say, Mr. Dignan," began Tony, "did you remember ——"

The banker broke in: "Of course! Don't you think a Troop Committee Man keeps his word!"

"Of course!" said Tony loyally.

The banker looked down at the bat Tony was carrying.

"Now tell me all about the game you just finished, Buddy. How many hits did you get?"

"Just one, sir, but it was a healthy beauty!" Tony launched into a rapid account of the homer with two on bases he got in the ninth inning. "That was my 'good turn' to-day, Mr. Dignan, going around those bases, for the winning run crossed the old plate when this Babe came home!" Tony patted his chest importantly.

"No; it wasn't your real 'good turn' to-day," said Mr. Dignan mysteriously. "Here's your corner, Tenderfoot. Hop out."

Tony got out, thinking Mr. Dignan said strange things sometimes. Anyway, his letter to North Carolina was on its way south. Tony looked about hopefully. He was glad Mr. Dignan had reminded him to do his "real" daily "good turn." He wanted to get it done before dark. He'd go directly into the house and see if he could not do to-day's for Mother.

A CHURCH UNDERGROUND

Let us, in imagination, make a journey to Rome and visit the Catacombs, where so many of the early Roman martyrs heard Holy Mass. Near the road we should find an opening leading by irregular steps to an underground gallery, sometimes more than forty feet below the surface. Often there are more steps leading to lower levels; two, three, and even four levels have been found.

At the bottom of the steps we should find long galleries cut in the tufa, with others branching off in all directions in such a maze that a guide would be necessary. Sometimes the galleries open into rooms of various sizes, and from time to time we should meet with air shafts like chimneys. Examining the walls we should see tombs on each side, frequently reaching from floor to ceiling.

Some of the rooms have one large tomb with an arch over it let into the wall at the end. These chambers are often decorated with pictures, as of the Good Shepherd, or the Blessed Virgin holding the Holy

Child, and sometimes with pictures which represent some mystery of our holy religion. For example, the drawing of a fish very often appears and always stands for Jesus Christ. The five letters of the Greek word for fish were made to stand for "Jesus Christ, Son of God, Savior." Often there are loaves and fishes and wine cups to tell us of the Blessed Sacrament. Other symbols that are common are the anchor, which because of the cross it showed, stood for hope, the palm for victory, the olive branch for peace.

Outside a number of tombs a small phial was discovered; at first it was supposed that this had contained blood and marked the resting place of the martyrs. The more common opinion now is that the vessels contained some strong smelling essence which was used to purify the air.

Some of the inscriptions on the tombs are very interesting, and a large number have been collected. I have copied out two which I thought you would like to read:

1. "Eutychius the father has erected this gravestone to his sweetest little son, Eutychianus. The child lived one year, two months, and four days. The servant of God."

2. "With the permission of his Pope, Marcellinus (296-304 A.D.), Severus the Deacon made in the level of the cemetery of Callistus, directly under that of the Pope, a family vault consisting of a double burial chamber with arched tombs and a shaft for air and light, as a quiet resting place for himself and his family, where his bones might be preserved in long sleep for his Maker and his Judge.

"The first body to be laid in the new family vault was his sweet little daughter, Severa, beloved by her parents and servants. At her birth God had endowed her for this earthly life with wonderful talents. Her body rests here in peace until it shall rise again in God, who took away her soul, chaste, modest and ever inviolate in His Holy Spirit. He, the Lord, will reclothe her at some time with spiritual glory. She lived a virgin nine years, eleven months, fifteen days. Thus was she translated out of this world."

There are so many Catacombs that if all the galleries were put in a straight line, it is said they would reach from one end of Italy to the other, and almost all were made by the Christians during the days of persecution.

Originally they were only used for burying the dead, but later on, when it was no longer safe for the faithful to meet for Holy Mass in the houses of the richer Christians as they had done at first, they made the rooms in the Catacombs larger and used them as churches.

Here at first the Christians were quite safe, and the Holy Sacrifice could be offered up in peace, for every spot where a dead body lay was under the special protection of Roman law and custom. But as time went on and the heathen found that the Catacombs were the churches of the Christians, they were often tracked there and put to death. They were forbidden to go there, and the openings were sometimes walled up.

When Constantine the Great became Emperor and the persecutions ceased, then the Christians began to build churches above ground, but for nearly a hundred years burials went on in the Catacombs, and people went down to them as to places of pilgrimage.

Just as our own days have seen a great increase in devotion to the Blessed Sacrament, so the fourth century was remarkable for the development of the veneration of the martyrs, and their bodies were removed from the Catacombs in large numbers and placed in the churches.

Little by little the Catacombs were forgotten and only in the sixteenth century were discovered afresh, but it is only in quite recent times that they have been opened up again and examined.

Now, if you ever go to Rome, you will be able to go down and pray on the very spots where many a martyr heard Holy Mass and received the Body of Christ which strengthened him to bear the worst his persecutor could do.

Sometimes when we are tempted to do wrong we could remember that the martyrs preferred torments and death to sin, and we might say with great earnestness this little text taken from the Holy Bible:

"Be thou faithful unto death, and I will give thee the crown of life."

HOW THE TOWER WAS SAVED

In the winter of 1662, a French fleet entered the harbor of Dunkirk, a seaport of France, which at that time belonged to England. The news soon spread; and before long the sailors and fishermen, followed by their mothers, wives and children, hurried to welcome their countrymen.

Then the people of Dunkirk learned that the King of France had bought back the town from the English. This seemed good news indeed, but the older and wiser men shook their heads sadly; they talked with their priest, and did not part till they had agreed to meet that night in his garden.

There was one woman in Dunkirk who had stayed at home, and when Bart, the fisherman, and his two boys reached their cottage, they found it bright and warm, with hot tea and brown cakes awaiting them.

"Why, what is the matter?" asked Bart's wife. "Have you lost your appetites in the open air? Dunkirk again belongs to France; this ought to be good news."

"So it would be," answered her husband, "were it not part of the bargain that every public building must be cut down till it is no higher than the highest dwelling. No one cares for the fortress—that can go; but to see the old church tower torn down almost breaks my heart. Why, the light from that tower has flashed out on the waters, guiding sailors and fishermen, since my grandfather's time. Who will dare now to cast a net? What vessel will dare come in now for a cargo? Tear down the tower, and Dunkirk is ruined."

Never before had the light in the church tower seemed to shine so brightly over the dark sea as it did that night. Within the chapel, the altar-lamp burned steadily as ever, its crimson light falling on the holy priest, who knelt at the altar praying for his people.

Silently, or talking in whispers, the fishermen gathered in the garden. Soon their pastor joined them, and then one plan after another was offered for saving the tower; but none was of use, and the meeting was about to break up, when Bart's younger son, John, asked leave to speak.

"Speak, my son," said the priest. "The wisdom of God has often been kept from the great and made known to the little ones."

"Father," answered John, "since no public building may be higher than the highest dwelling, there is only one way to save the tower; let a dwelling be made of the same height. Tear down our cottage to-morrow night, and before morning breaks build it as high as the top of the church tower; thus will the tower, the city and the fisheries of Dunkirk be saved."

It was all the priest could do to keep the men quiet. "My children," said he, "you see how the good God protects you. As for you, my son," laying his hand on the head of the happy boy, "you will become famous, and your mother will be proud of you."

The following night the French commander gave a ball on board his ship, to which he invited the English officers, and while they enjoyed themselves, the common soldiers made merry on shore.

In the meantime the people were not idle. Piece by piece the cottage was carried to the priest's garden, where the women kept watch, while the men were hard at work.

Within the chapel, the good priest prayed. Now and then, as the sound of the hammers reached his ear, he asked a blessing on the strange work, but, more than all, he returned thanks to our Lord, who had whispered to a child the secret by which Dunkirk would be saved.

When morning broke, the rough fishermen joined in the hymn of praise sung by the priest of God, and the breezes bore their voices over the water. Standing on the decks of their vessels, the French and the English officers saw a fisherman's cottage reaching high in the air, even above the church tower. From its roof waved the flag of France, while through the open door could be seen Bart, the fisherman, with his wife and boys, joyful that the tower was saved.

John Bart, in time, became a brave and famous officer, proving the truth of the good priest's words.

A WHALE CHASE

Here is a thrilling story about whaling as it was done seventy years ago. Nowadays, of course, the harpoon is fired from a gun instead of being thrown by hand, and many other changes have taken place, but the pursuit of the big "fish" is as thrilling as ever.

Thirty days out from Hobart our vessel floated under an unbroken arch of pure blue sky. On the distant horizon rested the light trade-wind clouds, reflecting all the splendor of the rising sun. The quiet, dreamy beauty of the scene is indescribable. The helmsman felt it and leaned sleepily against the wheel. The officer of the watch shut his eyes to it and nodded on the skylight. I was resting with head and arms on the bulwarks, when from the topmost cross-trees a clear voice rang out, "There she spouts! Black-skin ahead! There, there she blows again!"

"Where away?" shouted the mate.

"Three points on the weather bow. Hurrah! There she breaches clean out! Single spouts—a school of sperms!"

The quiet people of the ship were wakened up as though they had all suddenly been shocked by electricity, and jumped about with wild activity. The captain rushed up half-dressed from his cabin, with one side of his face lathered and a little rivulet of blood trickling from the other. The men blocked up the fore hatchway and tumbled over each other in their eagerness to reach the deck.

Then followed rapid orders as rapidly executed. The ship, which had been slipping along under double-reefed topsail, foresail, and mizzen, was easily hove to. "Haul up the foresail! Back the mainyard! Pass the tubs into the boats. Bear a hand, and jump in! See the tackle falls clear. Ready?"

"Ay, ay, sir; all ready!"

"Lower away!"

The falls whizzed through the davit-heads; the men, already seated at their oars, struck out the instant the boats touched the water.

South Sea whalers may be distinguished at sea by their boats; they usually carry five, sometimes seven, hung over the side by tackles attached to wooden or iron cranes, called davits, the bow of each boat hanging from one davit, and the stern from another. The tackle falls are carefully coiled upon the davits so that they can be let go with a certainty of running clear; and to the bottom of the tackle-blocks are attached weights which instantly unhook them when the boat touches the water. The boats are of peculiar shape; made low, and of great beam amidships, they gradually taper towards each end. Head and stern are alike, each sharp as a wedge, and raised by a gentle curve which traverses the whole length of the boat.

The whale-boats, being made in this way, are nearly flat-bottomed in the middle, and have little hold of the water. Their light build, sharp stems and rounded sides give them great swiftness; and their width and low center of gravity cause them to be very safe. They are steered by a long and heavy oar, which passes through a rope strap attached to the stern-post. The long oar gives to the steersman great power over his boat, and enables him to alter her direction or to turn her round in far less time than if he used the common rudder. In the stern of the boat is fixed a strong round piece of timber called the loggerhead, to which the towing rope is affixed, and which also serves to check the line when fast to a whale. The head-sheets are covered in by a board having a circular cut on its inner edge, used by the harpooner as a support when in the act of striking.

The harpoon, or "iron," as whalers call it, is made of the very best wrought iron, so tough that it will twist into any shape without breaking. It is about three and a half feet in length, with a keen, flat, barbed point at one end, and at the other a socket, in which is inserted the point of a heavy pole or staff. The whale-line is firmly fastened to the iron itself, and then connected with the staff in such a manner that, when the blow is struck and the line tightens, the staff comes out of the socket, leaving only the iron in the whale. If this plan were not adopted, the heavy pole, by its own weight and its resistance to the water, would tear out the iron, and so we should lose the "fish." When in chase, the harpoon lies on the boat's head with its point over the stem, ready for immediate use. Two harpoons are often fastened to the same line.

Beneath the gunwale in the bows are several brackets, containing knives, a hatchet and a couple of lances. The whaler's lance somewhat resembles the harpoon, but instead of barbs, it has a fine steel blade, and is attached to a short hand-line.

In the stern, or sometimes in the middle of each whale-boat, is a tub. In this the line is coiled with the greatest care, as the least hitch when it is running out would probably turn the whole boat's crew into the water. The line, which though small is of great strength, passes along the whole length of the boat, between the rowers, and runs on a roller fixed into the stem.

The row-locks, in which the oars work, are muffled with rope matting. Every oar is fastened to the boat with a strong lanyard, so that when in tow of a whale it can be tossed overboard hanging by the lanyard and leave all clear for the line to run out. Some boats are fitted with iron row-locks that move on swivels; by these the oars can be brought parallel to the boat's length and yet remain shipped ready for use.

Another boat was lowered soon after we left the ship and pulled in our wake; she followed as a "pick-up boat" in case of accident. The ship, which had still a boat's crew and the idlers aboard, with yards braced sharp up, advanced to serve as a meeting place, and was laying a course nearly parallel with our own. The chief mate "headed" the boat in which I rowed, and we had with us the best boat-steerer in the ship. Both were anxious to be first "fast" to the first whale of the season.

Our tough ash oars of eighteen feet length bent and buckled with the strain. The boat sprang with each vigorous stroke and hummed through the water as a bullet through the air. The headsman standing in

the stern, with the peg of the steer-oar grasped in his
left hand, stamped and raved with excitement, throwing his body forward in sympathy with each stroke
and with the right hand "backing up" the after oar
with all his strength. At the same time he was en-
couraging and urging us to fresh exertions, making
the most absurd promises in case of success and
threatening the boat-steerer with all sorts of awful
consequences if he missed the whale.

By this time we were in sight of the school, and,
turning my head, I could distinguish several of the
low, bushy spouts of the sperm whale and catch an
occasional glimpse of a huge black mass rolling in the
water. But there was no time for thought. Another
boat was creeping up to us, and we were yet some
distance from the game.

The headsman grew more frantic. "Give way, my
sons! Lift her to it! Long strokes! Pile it on, my
hearties! Well done, Derwenters! There she blows
again! Twenty minutes more, and it's our whale."
Suddenly his face changed. "Turned flukes!" said
he. The whales had disappeared, and with peaked
oars we lay motionless on the water waiting their
return to the surface. In a few minutes a short gush
of steam and spray broke midway between the two
boats. Half a dozen long strokes. "Steady, my lads,

softly, so ho! Stand up!" and the boat-steerer, peaking his oar, took his place in the bows. "Into her! Starn all!" shouted the headsman.

Both irons were buried in the whale, which lay for an instant perfectly still, whilst we backed hastily. Then the great black flukes rose into the air, and the whale "sounded" or dived, the line running out of the tub, round the loggerhead at the stern and out at the head, with wonderful velocity. The wood smoked and cracked with the friction, and the boat's head sank under the pressure.

More than half the line was carried out before it slacked, and in the moment that it did so, we began to haul in again and coil away in the tub. But the "struck fish" quickly appeared, the force acquired in rising carrying him nearly clean out of the water. He was evidently "gallied," making short darts in different directions; but, as the boat approached, he started off at full speed.

The line was now checked by a turn round the loggerhead, and only allowed to surge out gradually. The boat's velocity became terrific. We were carried through the water at the rate of nearly twenty miles an hour. Our little craft swept on in a deep trough; a huge wave of foam rolling ahead of us and two green walls of water rising above the gunwale, threatening every moment to descend upon the boat, already half filled by the blinding spray.

But the huge animal to which our boat was harnessed soon tired of his labor; the line again slackened, and the monster lay on the surface, writhing in agony, snapping his enormous jaws, and furiously lashing with his tail. As we coiled away the line, and as the distance between us and our prey decreased, I will candidly own that I was as "gallied" as the whale itself and would have given my own share of him to be absent from the scene.

Habit accustoms a man even to whaling; but few men, when "fast" for the first time, feel altogether easy. Our headsman stood coolly in the bows, lance in hand, exclaiming: "Haul me up, and he's a dead whale! A hundred barreler! Lay me on, lads!" And with the boat's nose nearly touching, he plunged a lance repeatedly into its side.

The whale started ahead, but the keen weapon had reached its mark and he fell into the "flurry." This was a tremendous spectacle. The enormous animal, convulsed in the agonies of death, struck the waves with head and tail alternately, and vast sheets of water came flying from beneath the mighty blows, which sounded like cracks of thunder. At the same time, beyond the vortex, the light boat danced as if

in triumph at her victory; and yet her slight frame trembled and vibrated with each stroke.

In a short time the struggling ceased; the whale turned slowly over. We had then leisure to look about us. The other two boats were both fast to one "fish," and nearly out of sight to windward. The fourth boat had struck a whale, but lost him, from the irons having drawn, and she was now making towards us. Uniting our strength we took the prize in tow and turned our course towards the ship, eight or nine miles distant.

She was making a long stretch in the direction of the fast boats. It was afternoon when, with no better dinner than dry biscuit and water, and under a burning sun, we fastened our tow-line and commenced the weary dray—the hardest but the most welcome part of a whaler's labor. With scorched faces and blistered hands, we pulled steadily on, lightening our toil with many a chorus, making rough calculations of the value of our prize, and at nightfall reached the ship and lashed the whale firmly alongside by strong chains and hawsers.

GLOSSARY

ā as in face.
â as in dare.
ă as in act.
ä as in farm.
a̤ as in tall.
ē as in eve.
ĕ as in edge.
ẽ as in baker.
ī as in like.
ĭ as in fin.

ō as in old.
ô as in or.
ŏ as in oft.
ū as in huge.
ŭ as in up.
û as in burn.
ōō as in mood.
ŏŏ as in brook.
ou as in out.

---

ab-sorbed' (ăb-sôrbd'), deeply interested, engrossed.

ab-surd' (ăb-sûrd'), foolish, nonsensical.

a-chieved' (ă-chēvd'), performed, attained.

ac-knowl'edged (ăk-nŏl'ĕjd), conceded, admitted.

ac-quaint'ed (ăk-kwānt'ĕd), familiar with.

a-dapt'ed (ă-dăpt'ĕd), made suitable.

ad-vance' (ăd-văns'), moving ahead.

a-fore'said (ă-fôr'sĕd), named before.

ag'ile (ăj'ĭl), quick, nimble, active.

a-gog' (ă-gŏg'), alive with curiosity, eager.

ag'o-ny (ăg'ō-nĭ), extreme pain of mind or body; anguish.

al'ma-nac (al'mă-năk), a book or calendar g i v i n g facts about days of week, etc.

a-loft' (ă-lŏft'), on high

al'tered (al'tẽrd), changed, modified.

al-ter'nate-ly (ăl-tẽr'nāt-lĭ), first one, then the other.

an'ces-tors (ăn'sĕs-tẽrz), forefathers.

an'guish (ăn'gwĭsh), distress, misery, agony.

an'i-mated (ănĭ'-māt-ĕd), lively.

an-noun'cing (ăn-noun'sĭng), making known publicly.

anx'ious (ănk'shŭs), deeply concerned.

269

ap′pe-tite (ăp′pĕ-tīt), hunger for food.

ap-pre′ci-a′tion (ăp-prē′shĭ-ā′shŭn), regard, feeling the full value of.

ap-pren′tice (ăp-prĕn′tĭs), one bound by an agreement in return for instruction in a trade.

ar′mor (är′mēr), a protective covering of steel for the body for use in battle.

as′pi-ra′tions (ăs′pĭ-rā′shŭnz), brief prayers said in a breath.

as-say′ (ăs-sā′), try, attempt.

as-sist′ance (ăs-sĭst′ăns), help

as-sur′ed-ly (ă-shōōr′ĕd-lĭ), surely, certainly.

as-ton′ished (ăs-tŏn′ĭsht), surprised, amazed.

as-ton′ish-ing (ăs-tŏn′ĭsh-ĭng), surprising.

as-tute′ (ăs-tūt′), keen, shrewd.

at′mos-phere (ăt′mŏs-fēr), air.

at-test′ (ăt-tĕst′), bear witness to, give proof of

at-tired′ (ăt-tīrd′), dressed.

a-vert′ (ă-vērt′), prevent.

au-dac′i-ty (a̤-dăs′ĭ-tĭ), daring, boldness.

bade (băd), directed, ordered, requested.

ban-dit′ti (băn-dĭt′tĭ), highwaymen, robbers, outlaws.

bar′gain (bär′gĕn), an agreement, a compact, a contract.

barque (bärk), a small three-masted vessel.

bar′ter (bär′tēr), trade, exchange.

Basque (băsk), one of a people living near the Bay of Biscay.

be-guile′ (bē-gīl′), charm, tempt.

be-lat′ed (bē-lāt′ĕd), delayed.

be-wil′dered (bē-wĭl′dērd), confused, dazed.

bier (bēr), tomb.

boards (bōrdz), tables.

bound′ary (bound′ă-rĭ), limit.

bow′ers (bou′ērz), sheltered places made of boughs or plants.

brakes (brāks), thickets, places overgrown with bushes.

bra′zen (brā′zn), composed of or like brass.

brisk′ly (brĭsk′lĭ), quickly.

brows (brouz), foreheads.

buc′ca-neers′ (bŭk′kă-nērz′), pirates, sea robbers.

bulk′y (bŭlk′ĭ), large, of great size.

bul′lion (bŭl′yŭn), gold or silver for coins.

bur'den (bûr'dĕn), load, care.

burgh'ers (bûrg'ērz), citizens of towns.

cal'cu-la'tions (k ă l ' k ū - l ā '- shŭnz), estimations, reckonings.

cap'tives (kăp'tĭvz), prisoners.

cas-cades' (kăs-kādz'), anything like a waterfall.

Cat'a-combs (kăt'ă-kōmz), underground passages with side recesses for tombs.

cau'tious-ly (ka'shŭs-lĭ), carefully.

ca-vort'ing (k ă - v ŏ r t'ĭ n g), prancing around.

cel'e-brate (sĕl'ĕ-brāt), to honor with suitable ceremonies, to observe with honor.

ce-les'tial (sē-lĕs'chăl), heavenly, divine.

chaff (chăf), the husks of grain.

chant (chănt), song.

chaste (chāst), modest, pure.

civ'il (sĭv'ĭl), well-bred, respectful.

clus'tered (klŭs'tērd), gathered or collected in groups.

cob'bler (kŏb'blēr), one who mends boots or shoes.

cogs (kŏgz), teeth or projections on a wheel for transmitting motion.

com'et (kŏm'ĕt), a heavenly body with a bright head and a long luminous tail.

com-mand'ed (kŏm-mănd'ĕd), ordered.

com-mod'i-ties (k ŏ m - m ŏ d'- ĭ-tēz), goods, merchandise.

com-pan'ions (kŏm-păn'yŭnz), those in company with one.

com-pas'sion (kŏm-păsh'ŭn), pity, mercy.

com-pla'cent-ly (kŏm-plā'sĕnt-lĭ), satisfied, pleased with themselves.

com'pli-cat-ed (kŏm'plĭ-kā-tĕd), complex, not simple.

con-clud'ed (kŏn-klūd'ĕd), decided.

condemned' (k ŏ n - d ĕ m d'), doomed, pronounced guilty.

con'fi-dent (kŏn'fĭ-dĕnt), sure, self-reliant.

con'se-quen-ces (kŏn'sĕ-kwĕn-sĕz), results.

con-sid'er-a'tion (kŏn-sĭd'ēr-ā'shŭn), thoughtfulness, kindliness.

con-sult'ing (kŏn-sŭlt'ĭng), taking into consideration, having regard for.

con-sumed′ (kŏn-sūmd′), eaten
or drunk up, used up.

con-tract′ (kŏn-trăkt′), to
shrink.

con-triv′ance (kŏn-trīv′ăns),
device, invention.

con-trive′ (kŏn-trīv′), try, attempt.

con-ve.t′ing (kŏn-vĕrt′ĭng),
changing from unbelief to
faith in God.

con-vinced′ (k ŏ n - v ĭ n s d′),
caused to believe.

crag (krăg), a steep rock.

crave (krāv), long for, desire.

crim′son (krĭm′zŏn), red.

cro′cus (krō′kŭs), an early
spring flower, white, yellow
or purple.

crum′bled (krŭm′bld), broken
into small pieces, fallen to
decay.

crum′pled (krŭm′pld), crushed.
pressed into wrinkles.

cull (kŭl), gather.

cu′ri-ous (kū′rĭ-ŭs), strange,
unusual, inquisitive.

cur′rent (kŭr′rĕnt), in general use.

curt′sy (kûrt′sĭ), a slight,
respectful bending of the
knees by women or girls.

dam′sel (dăm′zĕl), maiden.

dan′gling (dăn′glĭng), hanging
loosely.

dart′ing (därt′ĭng), dashing,
starting suddenly.

debt (dĕt), that which we owe
to others.

de-cline′ (dē-klīn′), close, end.

deemed (dēmd), thought, considered.

de-ferred′ (dē-fĕrd′), post-
poned, delayed.

de-fi′ance (dē-fī′ăns), refusal
to obey, disregard.

deg′ra-da′tion (dĕg′rā-dā′-
shŭn), disgrace, shame.

de-gree′ (dē-grē′), rank, position in life.

de-lib′er-a′tion (d ē - l i b ′ ĕ r-
ā′shŭn), the act of considering carefully.

de-mands′ (dē-măndz′), re-
quests, claims.

de-plor′a-ble (dē-plōr′ă-bl),
sad, lamentable.

de-ranged′ (dē-rānjed′), insane
mad.

des′per-ate (dĕs′pĕr-āt), without hope, frantic, reckless,
extremely dangerous, furious.

de-spise′ (dē-spīz′), to look
down upon, to spurn.

des′ti-na′tion (dĕs′tĭ-na′shŭn),
the place one has selected

for the end of a journey.

de-ter'mi-na'tion (dē-tēr'mǐ-nā'shǔn), purpose, firmness, resolution.

dig'ni-ty (dǐg'nǐ-tǐ), stateliness, nobleness.

dil'i-gent-ly (d i l ' ǐ - j ě n t-lǐ), working steadily, industriously.

dis-ci'ples (dǐs-sī'plz), those who believe and practice the teachings of another.

dis-com'fit-ed (dǐs-kǔm'fǐt-ěd), perplexed, ill at ease.

dis-dain' (dǐs-dān'), scorn, contempt, a feeling of dislike.

dis-tinct'ly (dǐs-tǐnkt'lǐ), clearly.

dis-tin'guish (dǐs-tǐn'gwǐsh), to see or discern clearly.

dis-tress' (dǐs-trěs'), p a i n, trouble, worry.

dis-trib'u-ted (dǐs-trǐb'ū-těd), dispensed, dealt out.

dole (dōl), a charitable gift of food or money.

doubt'ed (dout'ěd), was uncertain, questioned.

down'cast' (down'kȧst'), downhearted, sad.

dun'geon (dǔn'jǔn), a prison.

dusk (dǔsk), twilight, the end of daylight.

du'ti-ful (dū'tǐ-fǔl), obedient.

ear'nest-ly (ẽr'něst-lǐ), sincerely, solemnly.

e-lapse' (ē-lǎps'), pass.

em-bar'rass-ment (ěm-bǎr'rȧs-měnt), shame, uneasiness.

em'blem (ěm'blěm), sign, symbol.

en-coun'ter-ing (ěn-koun'tẽr-ǐng), meeting unexpectedly.

en-dowed' (ěn-doud'), f u r-nished with, enriched with.

en-raged' (ěn-rājd'), angry.

en'sign (ěn'sīn), banner, flag.

en'ter-prise (ěn'tẽr-prīz), undertaking, task of importance or of risk.

en'ter-tained' (ěn'tẽr-tānd'), received, and treated as guests.

es'sence (ěs'sěns), a perfume.

e-ter'ni-ty (ē-tẽr'nǐ-tǐ), immortality, life after death.

ev'i-dence (ěv'ǐ-děns), proof.

ex'e-cu'tion-ers (ěks'ě-kū'shǔn-ẽrz), those who put to death by authority, headsmen.

ex-haust'ed (ěgz-ȧst'ěd), worn out by exertion, weakened.

ex-pand' (ěks-pǎnd'), t o spread, to distend.

ex'qui-site (ěks'kwǐ-zǐt), rare, choice.

ex-traor'di-na-ry (ěks-trôr'dǐ-ně-rǐ), unusual, remarkable.

faint′est (fānt′ĕst), slightest, least.

fa-mil′iar (fă-mĭl′yẽr), well-known.

fam′ine (făm′ĭn), great scarcity of food, starvation.

fared (fârd), journeyed.

fer′vent (fẽr′vĕnt), earnest, ardent.

fête (fāt), a festival or holiday, usually celebrated out-doors.

file (fīl), a line of persons.

fil′lets (fĭl′lĕts), narrow bands worn across the forehead to hold the hair in place.

flar′ing (flâr′ĭng), fluttering as a flame, blazing.

flax′en (flăks′ĕn), pale yellow, resembling flax.

fleet′er (flēt′ẽr), quicker, swifter.

flock (flŏk), a congregation, members of a church.

fod′der (fŏd′dẽr), food for cattle or sheep; as, grass, hay.

frag′ments (frăg′mĕnts), pieces, particles.

fret′ful (frĕt′fŭl), peevish, irritable.

fric′tion (frĭk′shŭn), act of rubbing one thing against another.

funds (fŭndz), money.

gal′lied (găl′lēd), frightened.

gaz′ing (gāz′ĭng), looking steadily at.

gen′try (jĕn′trĭ), people of education and good birth.

gird′-ed (gẽrd′ĕd), encircled, bound.

gir′dle (gẽr′dl), belt.

glance (glăns), a quick, passing look of the eye.

glare (glâr), to shine dazzling-ly.

glee (glē), joy, happiness.

glim′mered (glĭm′mẽrd), glowed.

gloom′i-ly (glōōm′ĭ-lĭ), sulkily, sullenly.

glo′ri-ous (glō′rĭ-ŭs), full of honor.

gor′geous (gôr′jŭs), splendid, glittering in various colors.

grad′u-al-ly (grăd′ū-ăl-lĭ), slowly, by degrees.

grate′ful-ly (grāt′fŭl-lĭ), thankfully.

grave (grāv), serious, sedate.

grav′i-ty (grăv′ĭ-tĭ), serious-ness.

griev′ous (grēv′ŭs), distressing, sorrowful.

gruff (grŭf), rough, harsh.

grum'bled (grŭm'bld), complained, found fault.

guil'ders (gĭl'dērz), a piece of Dutch money worth about 40 cents.

gun'wale (gŭn'wāl; commonly gŭn'něl), the upper edge of the side of a vessel.

gur'gling (gûr'glĭng), bubbling, as of water flowing among pebbles.

ha'lo (hā'lō), a bright ring of light surrounding the heads of saints or holy persons.

har'le-quin (här'lĕ-kĭn or kwĭn), many-colored.

har-mo'ni-ous (här-mō'nĭ-ŭs), peaceable.

hea'then (hē'thn), pagan, one who does not acknowledge God.

hedge (hĕj), a border of bushes.

helms'man (hĕlmz'măn), a man who steers the vessel, a steersman.

her'alds (hĕr'ăldz), messengers of a king.

her'mit (hĕr'mĭt), one who lives alone and shuns society.

hilt (hĭlt), the handle of a sword or dagger.

hom'i-ly (hŏm'ĭ-lĭ), a sermon.

ho-ri'zon (hō-rī'zŭn), the line where sky and earth or water seem to meet.

hos'tage (hŏs'tāj), a person delivered to an enemy as a pledge.

hue (hū), color.

hus'ky (hŭs'kĭ), hoarse.

i'dol (ī'dŏl), an image of a being or a god used as an object of worship.

ig'no-min'i-ous (ĭg'nō-mĭn'ĭ-ŭs), humiliating, degrading.

im-ag'i-na'tion (ĭm-ăj'ĭ-nā'-shŭn), mental picture, fancy.

im-per'ti-nent-ly (ĭm-pĕr'tĭ-nĕnt-lĭ), saucily, disrespectfully, insolently.

im-plored' (ĭm-plôrd'), entreated, begged.

im'pro-vised (ĭm'prō-vīzd), made up on the spur of the moment.

in-ces'sant-ly (ĭn-sĕs'sănt-lĭ), unceasingly, without stopping.

in-creased' (ĭn-krēst'), grew, became greater.

in'de-scrib'a-ble (ĭn'dē-skrīb'-ă-bl), incapable of being described.

in-dig′nant (ĭn-dĭg′nănt), feeling anger.

in-dul′genced (ĭn-dŭl′jĕnsd), carrying remission of punishment.

in-gen′ious (ĭn-jēn′yŭs), clever, shrewd.

in-scrip′tions (ĭn-skrĭp′shŭnz), engravings, writings.

in-su′per-a-ble (ĭn-sū′pĕr-a-bl), unconquerable, not to be overcome.

in-tend′ed (ĭn-tĕnd′ĕd), meant, planned.

in-trud′er (ĭn-trōōd′ẽr), one who forces his way in without welcome or invitation.

in-vi′o-late (ĭn-vī′ō-lāt), pure, chaste, not defiled.

in-voke′ (ĭn-vōk′), to address in prayer.

ir-reg′u-lar (ĭr-rĕg′ū-lẽr), not straight, not uniform.

knead (nēd), to mix, usually with the hands, as dough.

lam′bent (lăm′bĕnt), softly radiant.

land′scape (lănd′skāp), a section of land seen in one view.

lan′yard (lăn′yẽrd), a piece of small rope.

launched (lȧncht), started out, set forth.

loy′al-ly (loi′ăl-lĭ), with faithfulness.

lug′ging (lŭg′gĭng), pulling, dragging.

lu′mi-nous (lū′mĭ-nŭs), giving forth light.

lus′cious (lŭsh′ŭs), delicious, delightful to the taste.

lus′ti-ly (lŭs′tĭ-lĭ), full of life and vigor, robustly.

mag-nif′i-cent-ly (măg-nĭf′ĭ-sĕnt-lĭ), splendidly.

mag′ni-fied (măg′nĭ-fīd), made more important, praised highly.

maimed (māmd), injured, disfigured, deprived of a necessary part.

man′na (măn′na), food divinely provided.

marsh′es (märsh′ĕz), swampy tracts of land.

mar′tyrs (här′tẽrz), those who are put to death for their religion.

mar′vel (mär′vĕl), wonder.

mar′vel-ous (mär′vĕl-ŭs), causing wonder.

math′e-mat′ic-al-ly (măth′ĕ-măt′ĭk-ăl-lĭ), exactly.

maze (māz), a network of paths, a labyrinth.

mead (mēd), meadow.

me-an'der-ing (mē-ăn'dēr-ĭng), winding.

mech'an-ism (měk'ăn-ĭzm), the the arrangement of the parts of a machine.

meek (mēk), mild of temper, piously humble.

meer'schaum (mēr'sham), a pipe made of fine white mineral of this name.

mem'o-ra-ble (měm'ō-rǎ-bl), worthy of remembrance, notable.

Mer'cu-ries (mēr'kū-rēz), Mercury was the messenger of the gods, noted for his speed in running.

min'strel (mĭn'strěl), a traveling poet and singer.

mir'a-cles (mĭr'ǎ-klz), marvels, wonderful acts beyond our understanding.

mi'ter (mī'tēr), a crown or headdress.

mock'ing-ly (m ŏ k ' ĭ n g - l ĭ) scornfully, tantalizingly, derisively.

moor (mōōr), a broad tract of waste land covered with heather.

mor'sels (môr'sělz), small quantities, little pieces of food.

moult'ing (mōlt'ĭng), shedding or renewing feathers.

moun'tain pas'ses (moun'tĭn pas'sěz), narrow roads or cuts through mountains.

mul'ti-tude (mŭl'tĭ-tūd), a crowd, a large number.

mys'ter-y (mĭs'tēr-ĭ), something secret or unexplained.

nec'es-sa-ry (něs'ěs-sā-rĭ), required, needed.

neck'er-chief (něk'ēr-chĭf), a kerchief or scarf about the neck.

nim'ble (nĭm'bl), quick and active, swift.

No'el (nō'ěl), Christmas; a Christmas carol; a shout of joy at Christmas time.

nook (nŏŏk), a corner, an out-of-the-way place.

ob-scured' (ŏb-skūrd), h i d-den.

ob-serv'ing (ŏb-sěrv'ing), taking notice.

ob'sta-cles (ŏb'stǎ-klz), those things that stand in the way, difficulties.

oc-cur′rence (ŏk-kŭr′rĕns), event, happening.

of-fend′ed (ŏf-fĕnd′ĕd), displeased, affronted.

of-fense (ŏf-fĕns′), a wrong, a crime.

om′i-nous (ŏm′ĭ-nŭs), threatening, foreboding evil.

o-rig′i-nal-ly (ō-rĭj′ĭ-năl-lĭ), in the beginning.

o′ver-tes′ty (ō′vẽr-tĕs′tĭ), unusually impatient or peevish.

pa-go′da-like (pă-gō′da-līk), resembling the tower-like buildings of the East.

pa-poose (pă-pōōs′), an Indian baby.

par′a-bles (păr′ă-blz), comparisons, short stories having a moral.

pas′sion (păsh′ŭn), a rage, anger.

pa-vil′ion (păvĭl′yŭn), a tent or shelter at an outdoor entertainment.

pe-cul′iar (pĕ-kūl′yẽr), strange, unusual, queer.

per′se-cu′tion (pẽr′sĕ-kū′shŭn), act of afflicting, punishing or putting to death because of religion.

per-sist′ed (pẽr-sĭst′ĕd), continued to say, persevered.

per′son-a-ble (pẽr′sŭn-a-bl), handsome.

per′son-al (pẽr′sŏn-ăl), relating to a particular person.

pe-ti′tion (pĕ-tĭsh′ŭn), request, entreat.

per-vades′ (pẽr-vādz′), fills, spreads through.

phi′al (fī′ăl), a broad, flat, shallow bowl.

pic′tur-esque′ (pĭk′tūr-ĕsk′), quaint, unusual.

pil′grim-age (pĭl′grĭm-āj), a journey to a sacred place.

pil′lars (pĭl′lẽrz), columns.

pip′pin (pĭp′pĭn), a kind of apple.

pit′e-ous (pĭt′ē-ŭs), sad, exciting sorrow.

plac′id (plăs′ĭd), calm, peaceful.

plain′tive (plān′tĭv), s a d, mournful.

plead′ed (plēd′ĕd), implored, begged.

plumes (plūmz), feathers.

pon′der-ous (pŏn′dẽr-ŭs), large, of great size.

por′tion (pôr′shŭn), share of an estate, marriage allowance.

port′ly (pōrt′lĭ), stout, stately in bearing.

pos'i-tive (pŏz'ĭ-tĭv), laid down. to be obeyed, leaving no doubt.

prec'i-pice (prĕs'ĭ-pĭs), a steep cliff.

prin'ci-ples (prĭn'cĭ-plz), definite rules of action.

pro-jec'tion (prō-jĕk'shŭn), that which juts out.

proph'et (prŏf'ĕt), one who foretells future events.

pro-por'tions (prō-pôr'shŭnz), dimensions, size.

pro-vi'sion (prō-vĭzh'ŭn), food

prowls (proulz), roams in search of prey.

Psalms (sämz), sacred songs in a book of the Old Testament.

pur-suit' (pûr-sūt'), chase.

quaint (kwānt), odd, unusual.

quest (kwĕst), a search.

quin'tal (kwĭn'tăl), a unit of weight varying in different countries from 100 to 200 pounds.

ra'di-ant (rā'dĭ-ănt), shining, brilliant.

raft'ers (răft'ĕrz), sloping timbers of a roof.

ra'pid-ly (răp'ĭd-lĭ), quickly.

ra-vine' (ră-vēn'), a long, deep hollow, a gully.

read'i-ly (rĕd'ĭ-lĭ), cheerfully, promptly, willingly.

re'al-ized (rē'ăl-īzd), felt keenly.

realm (rĕlm), a kingdom.

rea'son-ing (rē'zŭn-ĭng), act of thinking.

re-buked' (rē-būkd'), reprimanded, chided.

rec'og-nize (rĕk'ŏg-nīze), to identify as previously known.

Re-deem'er (rē-dēm'ĕr), Our Lord Jesus Christ.

re-flect'ed (re-flĕkt'ed), having the image returned as in a mirror.

re-flect'ing (rē-flĕkt'ĭng), throwing back.

re-joiced' (rē-joist'), was glad. expressed joy.

re-leased (rē-lēsd'), set free.

re-mon'strance (rē-mŏn'străns), protest, objection.

re-nown' (rē-noun'), fame, glory, honor.

re-sem'bles (rē-zĕm'blz), looks like, is similar to.

re-signed (rē-zīnd'), patiently uncomplaining, submissive.

res'o-lute (rĕz'ō-lūt), brave, firm, steadfast.

re-spect'a-ble (rē-spĕkt'ă-bl), decent.

re-splen'dent (rē-splĕn'dĕnt), brilliant, radiant.

re-spon'si-ble (rē-spŏn'sĭ-bl), accountable, liable.

re-store' (rē-stôr'), to return, to give back.

re-strain' (rē-strān'), to check, to hold.

Res'ur-rec'tion (rĕz'ŭr-rĕk'-shŭn), the rising of Christ from the dead.

re-vealed' (rē-vēld'), made known, disclosed.

rev'el-ry (rĕv'ĕl-rĭ), noisy merrymaking.

rev'er-ent-ly (rĕv'ĕr-ĕnt-lĭ), respectfully and with awe.

rev'er-ies (rĕv'ĕr-ēz), day dreams, deep musing or thought.

re-ward'ed (r ē w ạ r d ' ĕ d), showed appreciation, recompensed, paid.

roof'tree' (rōōf'trē), ridgepole of a roof; hence a roof, a family, a home.

rus'tics (rŭs'tĭks), peasants, country folk.

sa'bots' (să-bō'), wooden shoes.

sac'ri-ficed (săk'rĭfīsd) offered.

sac'ris-tan (săk'rĭs-tăn), a sexton.

sanc'tu-a-ry (săŋk'tū-ă-rĭ), a sacred place, that part of a church in which the main altar is placed.

sat'is-fac'tion (s ă t ' ĭ s - f ă k '-shŭn), contentment.

saun'tered (săn'tĕrd), strolled, walked slowly.

Ser'a-phim (sĕr'ă-fĭm), one of the choirs of angels.

shat'tered (shăt'tĕrd), broken into pieces.

shel'ter (shĕl'tĕr), a place of protection, refuge.

shel'tered (shĕl'tĕrd), p r o-tected.

shil'ling (shĭl'lĭng), a British silver coin ordinarily worth about twenty-four cents.

sig-nif'i-cant-ly (sĭg-nĭf'ĭ-cănt-lĭ), with meaning.

sin'ews (sĭn'ūz), tendons of muscles, cords.

site (sīt), place.

skim'mer-ing (skĭm'mĕr-ĭng), touching the surface lightly.

small'-clothes' (smạl'clōthz'), tight-fitting knee breeches as worn in the 18th century.

soared (sōrd), flew high into the air.

spe'cie (spē'shĭ), gold, silver or copper money.

spec-ta'tors (spĕk-tā'tẽrz), on-lookers, observers.

sprig (sprĭg), a small twig.

sprite (sprīt), an elf, a fairy.

stal'wart (stŏl'wẽrt), strong, sturdy.

stand'ard (stănd'ẽrd), emblem, flag, banner.

stew'ard (stū'ẽrd), one who manages the household of another.

sub'tle (sŭt'l), delicate, penetrating as a perfume.

suf-fi'cient (sŭf-fish'ĕnt), enough.

sulk'i-ly (sŭlk'ĭ-lĭ), sullenly, crossly.

sul'len (sŭl'len), sulkly, ill-humored.

sun'der-ing (sŭn'dẽr-ĭng), separating, dividing.

su-perb' (sū-pẽrb'), g r a n d, magnificent.

sur-passed' (sûr-păsd'), excelled.

swad'dled (swŏd'dld), wrapped or bandaged tightly.

tal'ents (tăl'ĕnts), abilities, gifts.

tank'ards (tănk'ẽrdz), large drinking vessels, usually with hinged covers.

tep-ee' (tĕp-ē'), a wigwam or tent of the A m e r i c a n Indians.

thatched (thăcht), covered with straw.

thrive (thrīv), grow.

throngs (thrŏngz), crowds.

to'ken (tō'kn), a sign or symbol.

tol'er-at-ed (tŏl'ẽr-āt-ĕd), put up with, endured.

tor'tured (tôr'tūrd), inflicted great pain or torment upon.

tot'tered (tŏt'tẽrd), shaken as if about to fall.

trag'ic (trăj'ĭk), sad, terrible.

trans-lat'ed (trans-lāt'ed), removed to Heaven without a natural death.

trans-par'ent (trăns-pâr'ĕnt), clear, capable of being seen through.

trea'cle (trē'kl), molasses.

tress'es (trĕs'ĕz), hair.

tric'kling (trĭk'klĭng), flowing gently, running in drops.

tri'fle (trī'fl), to toy with, to dally with.

tri'umph (trī'ŭmf), success, victory.

tu'fa (tū'fă), a porous rock.

tugged (tŭgd), pulled.

tu'nic (tū'nik), a loose-fitting garment.

tur'pen-tine (tûr'pĕn-tīn), the sap from pine trees.

tur'ret (tŭr'rĕt), a tower.

ty'rant (tī'rănt), an oppressive ruler.

un-com'fort-a-ble (ŭn-kŭm'fẽrt-ă-bl), uneasy, unpleasant.

un-daunt'ed (ŭn-dant'ĕd), fearless, bold.

un-leav'ened (ŭnlĕv'ĕnd), made without yeast, not raised.

un'slack'en-ing (ŭn'slăk'ĕn-ĭng), not slowing down.

un'suspect'ing (ŭn'sŭs-pĕkt'-ing), trusting, not aware of.

ut'most (ŭt'mōst), furthest.

vag'a-bond (văg'ă-bŏnd), rascal, a scamp, a wanderer.

vale (vāl), valley, low land between hills.

van'ish-ing (văn'ĭsh-ĭng), disappearing.

ve-loc'i-ty (vĕ-lŏs'ĭ-tĭ), speed.

ven'er-a-ble (vĕn'ẽr-ă-bl), revered, honored, old.

ven'er-a'tion (vĕn'ẽr-ā'shŭn), act of honoring, expression of reverent feeling.

ven'ture-some (vĕn'tūr-sŭm), daring, rash.

vi'bra-ted (vī'brā-tĕd), moved to and fro, wavered.

vi-cis'si-tude (vĭ-sĭs'sĭ-tūd), complete change of circumstances.

vig'or-ous (vĭg'ẽr-ŭs), strong, powerful.

vi'o-lence (vī'ō-lĕns), great strength or energy, fierceness.

vi'sion (vĭzh'ŭn), a dream.

vol-ca'no (vŏl-kā'nō), an opening in the earth's surface from which fire, rock and steam come forth.

vor'tex (vôr'tĕks), a whirlpool, an eddy.

wail (wāl), cry.

waist'coat (wāst'kōt), a vest.

ward'en (ward'n), a guardian, a keeper.

war'riors (war'yẽrz), soldiers, Indian braves.

wea'ry (wē'rĭ), tired.

wor'ship (wûr'ship), adore.

writh'ing (rīth'ĭng), twisting.

yawn'ing (yan'ing), gaping, opening the mouth wide.

yon'der (yŏn'dẽr), situated at a distance but still visible.

yore (yōr), long ago.

zeal (zēl), earnestness, ardor.